AF446865

"The Holy Spirit and a lot of education is behind Jerry's words. This book should be available in every church in America. God has blessed him with the power of compassionate communication."
—John D. Woodward, Professor of Business Adm. and Accounting, Polk State College

"I read this and loved it. I have served more than twenty years in the prison ministry with Jerry and observed firsthand how he helped the inmates/young men to recognize their desert experience, encouraging them each week with the presence of God and His holiness. The account of Moses and the burning bush would condition their hearts to receive God's Word and the message delivered without the many influences and distractions they would encounter even within the confinements of the prison walls. We saw many people healed, delivered, and set free. Hallelujah!"
—Kevin Whitmore, Retired Federal Prosecutor; Retired Captain, U.S. Navy JAG Corps; Founder, Last Chance Law Firm, PLLC

THE DESERT LOOK

DISCOVERING GOD'S REVELATION BEYOND WORLDLY INFLUENCE AND DISTRACTION

LARGE PRINT EDITION

JERRY ALLEN WOODWARD

Published by Innovo Publishing, LLC
www.innovopublishing.com
1-888-546-2111

Publishing quality books, eBooks, audiobooks, music, screenplays & courses for the Christian & wholesome markets since 2008.

THE DESERT LOOK
Discovering God's Revelation Beyond Worldly Influence and Distraction

Library of Congress Control Number: 2024923358
ISBN: 979-8-88928-052-1

Cover Design & Interior Layout: Innovo Publishing, LLC

Printed in the United States of America
U.S. Printing History
First Edition: 2024

CONTENTS

Part 3: For the Love of God

ACKNOWLEDGMENTS

I would like to acknowledge here those influential professors at Union University who challenged me in my faith and formed a lasting dedication in the pursuit of knowing and serving our Lord and Savior. They would inspire a continuing transformation, resulting in a Master and slave relationship throughout my faith journey. Knowing our Lord and not just knowing *about* Him would reveal His truths in a way of life that would usher in a freedom that easily escapes us.

I have the privilege to recognize my wife, Barbara, and my three children, Christine, Michael, and Katherine. They cannot fathom the influence they have had on me with their patience and perseverance. I have truly seen the fruit of the Spirit exceptionally blossom before their old dad. Each one is so very different yet the same in love and honor for Mom and Dad. The marriage of my two daughters has extended the family, and it is incomprehensible to grasp how God orchestrated such footsteps that have truly enriched my life, taking me down unfamiliar paths that have strengthened my faith. They know who they are, and the family keeps growing to the praise and honor of our Lord Jesus Christ.

And then there is John. Not the Apostle John, although the demonstrated encouragement is evident in likeness, but Cousin John. Our fathers were close brothers, designing, engineering, and building things together early in their lives. I grew up with three sisters, and so John would be like a surrogate brother. He certainly became a brother in Christ and has encouraged me throughout the pages of these chapters. Some suggest in faith that we need accountability partners, and I understand the reference; John has certainly been that over the years. But *partners* is a term I feel is best fit for the world's references, as relationships in Christ transcend such thought, and we become one in a body that is truly one. I thank John for his encouragement to complete this work and look forward to his continued encouragement in future endeavors for Christ and the church.

I am grateful, with a special thanks to Bart Dahmer, my publisher, and especially Rachael Carrington, senior editor—for her diligent work and masterful editing of this inspired work in order that it could be clearly communicated. It has been a most joyful journey into the publishing world.

PREFACE

MY STORY

It has been years that the burden to share the following pages with you has lingered. Where would be the time for me to sit quietly before the Lord and not become an *author* but simply a *voice* from the voice of the Lord. So rather than *author*, *messenger* is a title that feels much more appropriate. It took being forced into retirement by the company I was working for to guide me to where my heart was yearning; so you could say that yes, sometimes what seems so bad has the good He is desiring.

The following description of my early childhood and faith walk will be different, maybe greatly different than others. But it is the cultural environment I grew up in and a perspective that was lived and real. That does not make other experiences less or more meaningful because we know our God has no favorites. There are no prejudices or preferences, just a yearning for all

He has created to know Him, leading to a way of holiness that honors and glorifies Him.

Here is my story. My journey in life and in faith to this point is not unlike many who grew up in a Christian family in the 1950s, where virtually everyone on the block went to a neighborhood church, the streets were serenely quiet, virtually every business was closed (no, they weren't all Chick-fil-As), and families ate a Sunday meal that had begun preparation the day before. Special family time. You may remember, or if you are fortunate, you still enjoy, the traditional meal and family time. I would suggest, though, you would be in the minority.

We were in Sunday school, we met on weeknights for church fellowship, and friendships centered around the church family. Bible studies and lessons would prepare us for a Sunday review and discussion. Some of us would join choirs, and singing would be a service that many of us would make a long-term, if not lifetime, commitment. Those early years after World War II seemed to be classified with common denominators in work ethics, faith, and friendships. It seemed everyone went to church and knew about Jesus, at least in our circles of friendship and community.

There would come a time in my faith journey, though, when I would search myself (though the search was not mine) and my relationship with Jesus. If I were to count, I have read the Bible numerous times, and there are shelves of Christian (and philosophical) books I have read by well-known authors and writers. Daily journaling and prayer defined my morning workouts, and I even took on the challenge of a Christian studies master's program while working, traveling most of the time. I have sought knowing our Lord in many taught methods as well—listening to many expositions of His Word, observing theological concepts in discussion, and reading as much material I could possibly absorb, all contributing to my growth and maturing in the faith. As I would continue to grow, I knew there was more I wanted than what my traditional search methods were providing. Prayerfully I would ask for more, and that prayer would be simple: *Lord, draw me close to You that You would draw near to me and impart Your wisdom, knowledge, and understanding that I might grow and mature in my faith and become all that You desire in me and of me.*

That seeking would take me to a lonely place, and I would ponder the desert. I would not be in a physical desert, but it would be a place where worldly influences and distractions were void. It would be humbling, recognizing who He truly is and realizing who I was. His holiness would strip the sandals off my feet (figuratively, of course), and I would be in awe of His presence.

When Moses was taken into the desert by God, he went and was isolated from worldly influences and distractions and there encountered His Creator. His trek would unexpectedly encounter a defying of natural defining laws known to mankind, with a non-extinguishing fire and the reality of a voice known not from where. He would be humbled. He would listen, and he would obey.

That was the encounter and experience I so desired, and the revelation that would come so unexpectedly would drop subtle shackles from endless struggles and bring me to a new level of understanding of myself and who our God is. I have referred to it as a "Desert Look"—alone and beyond worldly influences and temptations. One that was necessary for me in relationship to give myself away to walk ever so close as a new wedded couple along the shores of the water of life.

THE DESERT LOOK

The Lord has built in everyone (in my opinion) a desire to search for the reason they are, the reason they exist. And many, me and you included, seek the One True God and search to know Him. We look down many avenues, we look in many ways, but until we remove nearly all of the world's influences, noises, and unruly temptations, we have a worldly, filtered vision that is cloudy at best. *The Desert Look* brings you alone to the revealing of our God, and it is an amazing look that defies worldly rationalizations and summations. Moses saw God's revealing in a burning bush that would not extinguish and in a voice that no one else could hear, revealing the holiness of God. That is the look that we need to get closest to: our God removing our sandals—maybe not physically from our feet but from the very fabric of our souls. It's a humbling experience and one that, in my mind, cannot happen without the desert experience. Hence, *The Desert Look*.

Therefore the overall goal for this book is to take you to that desert in search of what no one can fathom until we, ourselves, experience what surpasses our own expectations. This book is not that place and look, but it will hopefully lead you beyond the pages to be alone with God, letting Him reveal that eternal fire that will keep His light burning in your heart, finding Him closer and closer in your faith journey in life. It is a *Desert Look* that can be life-changing because of holy ground His presence alone can put under our feet.

It is my prayer that these pages would open up avenues of heaven that will take you far beyond what is written to reveal how holy and awesome our God truly is. The psalmist wrote,

"He provided redemption for His people, and ordained His covenant forever; Holy and awesome is His name" (Ps. 111:9). You may already know that is true, but continuing the search to know Him deeper and deeper will never leave one too saturated with the goodness of God; the more one seeks, the more He gives and gives endlessly.

The sections of this book walk you through this journey to the desert as you seek to know Him more intimately than you did before:

- *Part 1: Oh Know It's Him,* means that He knows me and accepts me, even with my . . .

- *Part 2: Dislocated Hip*, in His body.

- *Part 3: For the Love of God,* how can it be? But it is, and oh, how grateful I am that He accepts my adoration and my praise as I glorify Him.

As you read, take to the *desert*, my friends, and *look*. You will discover the unfathomable because our God is an amazing God who loves to reveal Himself in ways our world can never offer or explain. His love is beyond knowing; how deep, how wide, and how high, we cannot fathom—but He has promised such, and this is worth seeking, finding, and enjoying forever.

Be blessed, my friends. Be blessed.

PART 1:
OH KNOW IT'S HIM

Jeremiah 9:23-24

1

SEEKING THE UNIMAGINABLE

How is it that a lazy running creek forming a beautiful walk through the trees, not knowing or caring if and where it will end, can absorb the glory of the magnificent creation? Meandering through life, not always knowing where it will take us, can be a magnificent journey of enjoying our Creator God in all His glory.

Many years ago, General Electric had a pavilion (Imagination Pavilion) at Epcot Center in Orlando that was an exposition of the advancements of home technology, both historically and into the future. As a young child, I was enamored not by the innovations but by a mascot of a theme called "Figment"—a purple dragon influenced and created by the phrase, "Don't tell me this is a figment of my imagination." In the presentation of Figment are his aspirations to be something special— "I wish I could be"—and using his imagination to discover all kinds of new things. But as passing time would have it, Figment has faded to near extinction except for brief appearances on the screen. It seems not all imagination is relevant to our needs or has any chance of surviving the realities of life. Note this, though, the creation of Figment had a successful purpose beyond tantalizing the minds of children in search of the imaginable. The creation and marketing of Figment has generated millions of dollars for Disney and its stockholders, lest we ever forget the corporate purpose of entertaining our minds.

What about the *unimaginable,* though? And what purpose might something that is beyond our own imagination (no mind can conceive) have, not just for our future, but in our daily walk in life? How in the world can we grasp something that is inconceivable, let alone that it could be the very sustenance that is the difference between life and death?

We seldom think about things we cannot see or hear or smell or taste or feel. Our five senses try to dictate what we believe and guide decisions that reveal who we are. We can imagine what we might want to be as a child, seeking fulfillment in life, and we can diligently pursue those dreams and most often achieve them. But how do you pursue the unimaginable? How do you seek that which is beyond the human senses, and where does it lead? How would you know that you have achieved your destiny should you embark on such a journey? These are not invalid questions, and fortunately they are questions of old that have been answered for every age.

Wisdom, knowledge, and understanding are the bedrock of an unimaginable Creator

God. A God that wants you to know Him. A God that provides every detail needed to initiate that journey into the unknown and make it known. He created us to know Him, and by knowing Him, everything else falls into place and becomes a living sacrifice and act of worship. We find that everyone who has ever sought the unimaginable began a new journey, stepping out of the known and following unfamiliar and least-traveled paths.

Is it worth the venture? Hopefully the following pages will convince you to step out and begin the journey if you have not already headed into the forest with streams of living water. And if you are already long into the journey, you will find encouragement and an evolving confidence that truly reveals that you know your Creator, Sustainer, and Life Eternal beyond the imaginable.

2

MIND-BOGGLING

We catch a glimpse, maybe through the trees, of the night sky that is lighted bright by a light that is not its own. It's not day, and it's not the sun, and we reflect on what we know is more and not seen.

Think about this. I have!

It is estimated that there are one hundred fifty to three hundred billion galaxies in just the observable universe alone, and in each galaxy, for context, there are billions of stars—three hundred billion in our own galaxy, the Milky Way. I don't know about you, but that is more Milky Ways than our entire population could eat in a lifetime. When Carl Sager was asked how many stars there were, his response of billions and billions may have been well short of reality in the true universe.

Our Lord's response to Abram when Abram was questioning Him about having offspring that had yet been provided is truest of all assessments, and all we need to know from an awesome and amazing God:

> *And He took him outside and said, "Now look toward the heavens [go ahead, you look too, and hopefully on a clear night], count the stars, if you are able to count them. (Gen. 15:5)*

Now, granted, Abram didn't have a Hubble telescope to see what astronomer scientists estimate we can: about one twenty-fourth-millionth of the sky. But even with our current technology, we still cannot count all the stars.

It is worth repeating: *Think about this.* And for all those who say that this stuff just happened, well, think about that too! That may not be amazing enough for some, so here is the caveat: in all of our searching, wanting to find any sign of life outside of our position of great privilege, we have found none. That doesn't necessarily mean there isn't any far beyond what we can see and find in all of the stars. Even Billy Graham once said when asked about life on other planets that somewhere out there, God may have created the very privilege He has given us. That certainly doesn't diminish the rarity of our blessing to live, and yes, to know our Creator and the Creator of the entire universe.

A privilege such as this, and we find ways to criticize, argue, fight, and war amongst ourselves. Why? Many might just scratch their heads for that ageless *question*. But for me, the answer seems simple. Where are our eyes looking? Where is our focus? Where is our heart? Does our gaze look to the heavens and the One who created it all, everything in and of existence? Do we belong to anyone beyond ourselves? Don't be quick to answer that; pause and think about the mountains of cries:

> *My body*
> *Mine, mine, mine*
> *Get your own*
> *I worked hard for this*
> *Laissez faire*
> *I will do what I want; it's what I want*
> *It's time I did something for myself*
> *I will decide for myself*

This is just a sampling to get you thinking, and for many of us we can relate at some time in our lives to these, and others you may have thought of. That's our nature, our natural selves, ourselves. None of us escape these natural tendencies, and when we find ourselves caught in related circumstances, some of us have heard this response from those who have been privileged to be around us in such times: *Who died and made you God of the universe?*

So much to think about, especially the tendency to want to be our own god. There was one angel in particular, and many accompanying, that were cast out of heaven's home for this very reason, and they prowl around, wanting more and more company to grieve the God of all creation. Yes, the Creator of the heavens and earth and all that is within brings us back to the amazing, mind-boggling God He is.

When you have a definitive count of the stars, please let me know. When you give up trying, please let me know; we have much in common. We don't have one who died and made us god of the universe, but we have One who died and provided that we might live forever with Him in a place that is mind-boggling and beyond our imagination, an amazing place where every tear will be wiped away, and there will no longer be any death, nor mourning, nor crying, nor pain, for first things will have passed away (Rev. 21:4). That is beyond our imagination, beyond our scope of understanding, and even brings tears to one's eyes—a hope beyond all hope. But that is my home. That is your home, and we all are on a journey with a destiny in the heavens, should we so choose.

This God of our creation said, "Behold, I set before you the way of life and the way of death" (Jer. 21:8). This isn't in the context of the setting, but I don't think it is too much of a stretch to bring to mind the truths of the gospel message our Lord brought to earth:

> *"I am the resurrection and the life, he who believes in Me will live even though he dies, and everyone who lives and believes in Me will never die. . . . Do you believe this?" (John 11:25-27)*

That was and is the question of our Lord Jesus Christ.

> *Blessed is a man who perseveres under trial; for once he has been approved, he will receive the crown of life which the Lord promised to those who love Him. (James 1:12)*

> *When Christ, who is our life, is revealed, then you also will be revealed with Him in Glory. (Colossians 3:4)*

> *Many of those who sleep in the dust of the ground will awake, these to*

everlasting life, but the others to disgrace and everlasting contempt. (Daniel 12:2)

"Truly, truly, I say to you, he who hears My word, and believes Him who sent Me, has eternal life, and does not come into judgment, but has passed out of death into life." (John 5:24)

"Do not let your heart be troubled; believe in God, believe also in Me. In My Father's house are many rooms; if it were not so, I would have told you; for I go to prepare a place for you, and if I go and prepare a place for you, I will come again and receive you to Myself, that where I am, there you may be also, and you know the way where I am going." (John 4:1-4)

3

NO CHOICE BUT CHOICE

We have chosen one without a choice from a depth of love that is known but cannot be explained.

There are many roads in life that can be taken, some leading to fast lanes crowded with others that are racing on a journey of purpose, others leading to isolated country roads that are dotted with picturesque scenery that widens our thoughts of staying around and not venturing on. And then there are those that beckon us to travel but leave us at an unanticipated dead-end without knowing how we got there or where to go from there.

Sometimes we approach crossroads without a real map of the destiny that awaits the unseen, and we use interesting methods to decide which path to take. Either way makes it difficult, if not impossible to return and try the other way, which increases the dissonance to a level where the threshold can be debilitating.

Ah, the decisions, and they must be made to go on. Staying doesn't really happen in life, for we are pulled along even if reluctant to move. Think about it: You may be where you were twenty-five years ago (although unlikely these days) physically, but you are not the same. Things have changed—what you look like, what you are doing, what you are interested in (new or not) that has garnered your time. Does anything remain the same? Well, the basics of some things can remain the same, but the seasoning has modified the starches of life's carbohydrates, and the maturing has either ripened the fruit of our labor or left us rotting away, losing the ripened taste we should be destined for.

The interconnected webs that ladder in the space between heaven and earth are most important for our spirits, and the spiritual experiences open the highway that leads to heaven's reward of relationship with the Builder. The sticky substance of knowledge holds us intact as we traverse the many directions that lead closer and closer to the source of identity that has no equal. It is a destiny of purpose that leads us amongst others seeking the same path of spiritual enrichment.

We ask many things during our journey to help ensure the choices we make are ones that benefit and reward us, with joyful song and peace that allows a breath of freshness to accompany the steps we take. We have no choice but to choose as the days turn to nights and light and darkness come with the passing time. How do we know what will be right and what will be wrong? Many times, that assuredness of the right finds us in the wrong. Deep in our hearts are answers that evade us because of subtle distractions we often don't even recognize. *We know, but we don't*, would be a profitable assessment. *We know we are pleasing You, Lord. Right? We are doing what You have asked us to do; we are sure because we have been told. But for what purpose do we endeavor? What true motive stands as the bedrock?*

You have said, Lord, "Therefore I urge you brethren to offer your bodies as a living sacrifice, holy and pleasing to the Lord, for this is your spiritual service of worship."[1] So sacrifice is required, right? And we have read of the required sacrifices and instituted them in our designs of worship. The method—has it become our king? Or is the King of kings still in sight that we can see what is to be seen, and we bring our offerings, though not burning, on the altar of the sacrifice?

Is this pleasing to You, Lord? We are sure it is until the convicting voice—the small, quiet voice that is pounding a rhythm in our hearts that says, *Delight in Me, my child. Delight in me. Let the desires of your heart be Me; I will give you Me.*

Do I really delight in Your sacrifices and Your offerings? asks the Lord. Truly asking oneself, *Where is my loyalty in this? Do I really know You, Lord? What knowledge do I have of You rather than burnt offerings? You said, "For I delight in loyalty rather than sacrifice, and in knowledge of God rather than burnt offerings"* (Hosea 6:6). *Those are Your words, Lord. Shall I come to know You that You would make me yours! I have no choice but to choose. If I do not choose, then I have chosen, and if I do choose, I have also chosen.*

Behold, You set before us the way of life and the way of death.[2] It is a road that has to be taken. There is no other way. It is the determinant crossroads. You know the plans You have for us. You have declared it. They are plans to prosper us and not to harm us. Plans to give us hope and a future. They are Your plans, not ours, though we often think that we have our destiny in hand when it is Your hand that holds our future, our destiny.

You have all the cards, and You know when to hold them and when to fold them. You knew us before our beginnings, and You know our ends.

We can choose, but we really have no choice in the matter. We did not choose the beginning, and the end will come. It is defined, and it is definite. That You set before us the way of life or the way of death seems to elude a choice, and rightly so, but it is You that has chosen to offer us only one or the other; there is no other option, there is no other choice. There is Choice, but really no choice.

4

THE FOREST
AND THE TREES

Look at the trees—how crooked their deformity. Should they not be cut down, for soon the trunk would straighten and reach its true delight? From the top, revel in the uniqueness; what seemed to be loss is gain.

The previous chapter revealed that there are paths we can take in life, and sometimes it feels like we are heading into a forest that is pretty scary—with huge trees that let in little sunlight. But stopping and isolating a tree in our vision and following it to its highest point, though feeling ominous, reveals a life lesson that can be the difference between life and death. We find that though the tree's trunk may be bent in more than one direction, curving this way and then back, it is the life of the tree and its journey in growth—the light through the forest of many trees as it continually seeks the source of its nourishment and growth.

We, too, seek the source of our nourishment and growth, and it is found in the Light of the World. It is a continuous search, and there will be many obstacles to crowd out the light and dim our vision. But we lean this way and that way on Him, and He guides us to the light. Though our path has seemed all but narrow and straight looking back, we still have the light in our vision and are drawing nearer than before.

Look to the trees and see their search for the light. Look at the many different trees and their paths; they are all seeking the light. Though they look very different, they are the same; they all want the nourishment that provides for their growth, and they all find it from the same source—the light of the world that is from the Light of the World.

Now we know that you can have trees without a forest, but you cannot have a forest without trees. Where am I going with this? Well, this is where your creative minds are challenged to determine its essence, and it is for you alone. The world has both scenarios and a question to ask: Which, to you, is grander? Would you prefer to stare at the apple tree that Washington chopped down (some infer that was a story made up) or walk through the Redwood Forest amongst the Sequoia sempervirens trees, which are the tallest and most grand trees on earth—closer to its source of life than any other?

Put me in the Forest and let me gaze at the top of those trees. It is amazing to see such enormity and then just think, when have you reached your pinnacle? Will others be amazed at your enormity in the forest and gaze to where the light has come from for you to grow to such stature?

A tree alone may be grand, but true grandeur will not be found but in the midst of many. It is nature at its best, and your nature is found amongst others, not alone by yourself. It is your surroundings that bring out your nature, grand or not. Those who choose to walk amongst you, though through scary places at times, are ones that see your grandeur in a source of light that never dims and shines before all men because of your good deeds when you intentionally serve the Lord.

The trees of the forest "experience life-giving light" and are never in darkness that lasts. We, too, can "experience life-giving light . . . and never walk in darkness."[3] That is a claim and a promise that will offend some who will suggest you are boasting; that it is only your word. That is why we seek out the trees and the forest that validates our grandeur.

5

EMERGING WATERS

Look at the water—seemingly from nowhere, welling up and cascading and gushing over an entire body from head to toe, unrestrained. You can hardly stand up from the push to move forward in its washing.

The earth was formless and void, and darkness was over the surface of the deep, and the Spirit of God was moving over the surface of the waters. (Gen. 1:2)

Could anyone title a chapter "Emerging Waters," for even in the beginning when the earth was formless and void, there was water? It did not come into being; it was there—important and prominent, known and established.

Why would that be important? There is one and only one most important thing that scientists and astronomers search for when combing the heavens, galaxies, and planets in search of life other than our own here on Earth—any current or past sign or form of water. They are convinced that without water, no life form can exist that we know of or have been told of or has been revealed in any fashion of knowledge.

So, let's not focus on the beginning of Creation and focus on simply a new beginning, a new formation transitioning from the old. That is exactly what happens during an accepted baptism. A new identity is pronounced and witnessed, and water symbolizes what has transpired by the power of the Holy Spirit.

The scene at the River Jordan is an immersion under the water and an emerging from the water that drips, even flows from the top of the head over the entire body in a flushing action that is exhilarating to witness and is clearly seen. Tears of joy flow from the baptized and even those watching because of the magnitude of what has happened—buried and raised to walk in new life. Water carried up out of the river, emerging with the baptized, while the glistening sun (Son) reflects its rays in every drop. If ever a voice was to be heard with the clamoring of singing and dancing of angels in celebration, the shout of response would be, *Here am I, Lord! Here am I.*

How prominent is the water for a new believer, or even the most seasoned? The Apostle John, inspired, wrote down an answer Jesus gave to Nicodemus when he was perplexed regarding the rebirth of a man and directly questioned the Lord. Jesus, answering him, said, "Truly, truly, I say to you, unless one is born of water and the Spirit he cannot enter into the kingdom of God."[4] You could say, *Open the floodgates of heaven; I'm coming in with water springing up to eternal life.*

It is by water that new things are formed. Peter wrote that "in the last days when mockers will come with their mocking, following after their own lusts, saying, 'where is the promise of His coming?'"[5] That was heralded by all believers—that Jesus is coming again (and for good reason). Writing further, he said, "When they maintain this, it escapes their notice that by the word of God the heavens existed long ago, and the earth was formed out of water and by water."[6]

Yes, emerging water from water that exists. How can it be? For you who have been baptized, you know. For those of you who are looking forward, you will know. For you who refuse to come to the water, it is impossible to know. A door of knowledge that surpasses all understanding is opened, and a new beginning is born. A new relationship is in formation, and eyes are widened with an amazing assurance of things hoped for and a conviction of things not seen. Oh, the water, oh, the washing, oh, the cleansing . . . everything made new. And the shekinah glory of the Lord shines like never before as the Lord is now present in this newly created temple by the given Holy Spirit, and I say, *We all who believe, say, "Hallelujah!"* This water is never stagnant; it is an ever-flowing, eternal river from the innermost being. By Jesus' own words, we know this to be true, for He said, "He who believes in Me, as the Scripture said, 'from His innermost being will flow rivers of living water'"[7]

Yes, emerging water now overflowing, flowing freely to be received by all those who believe, and the river flows! Flowing here and there, wherever He may go as we follow Him. There isn't an ocean too deep or a mountain too high; He is followed by those who believe, and this emerging, living water flows endlessly, for the source is infinite. The more that is received, the more that is given.

6

BY THE WAY— LEFT BEHIND

While watching over all creation, one may not know, but they have been left behind until they find a way back to the path.

I am burdened, often thinking about the rich in the world and what seems to be a pattern of response in belief or not, and what is seen that truly proves a case for belief.

There are numerous accounts in the Bible that set our minds in rhythm with the measurement that finds its judgment in heaven. We are flooded daily with worldly accounts of successes that formulate beliefs that in no way are found in failure. Rewards are only found in achievement and many times at the expense of another's measured failure.

The question becomes, who is left behind? If you are considered first in achievement, then everything else is left behind. And there is an accompanying and binding companion of identity: by what way did you travel to get to where you arrived?

I would like to share one of the biblical accounts that may be perplexing to many that relates to all that we do to make sure the way we travel results in our best interest and benefit.

Matthew wrote in his Gospel about a young man, a rich ruler, who felt he had earned what all desire (or at least in good sense, should desire): to go to heaven one day with life that is eternal. Rhetorically (I'm pretty sure) he asked, "What good thing shall I do that I may obtain eternal life?" (Matt. 19:16). The question personifies common thought about what we must do and evades the truths about what another had to do that we could not do for ourselves.

Our Lord was just as rhetorical in His response to the question, and He answered with a question. (I have to digress here on another thought. We might consider our Lord's strategy when questioned about things we know and should be known by the questioner so that you can drive them to a deeper understanding that challenges their postulate. But back to the shared Gospel account.) Jesus' question in response was, "Why are you asking Me about what is good?" (Matt. 19:17)—knowing, I'm sure, the man felt he was a *good person*. But if you wish, He continued, "Keep the commandments," for which we know has proven impossible. The young man presses, "Which ones?" Our Lord enumerates six commandments that I believe He knew the young ruler had kept, which led to his response: "All these things I have kept; what am I still lacking?" Now there was more to this, and the young ruler was about to find out, in a way that would be unexpected—a test of the heart, if you will—what it is that truly motivated this man in his endeavors, his search for the eternal reward, his loyalty. Maybe the young ruler expected Jesus to answer in confirmation, stating, "Nothing, if you have kept these. Well done." But He didn't, knowing what was standing in the way of an eternal reward. He would respond with a question of the heart, searching for what was most important and valuable: "If you wish to be complete."

Have you ever thought about that in your own aspirations, in your own life? It beckons the thought, *What am I missing in life? Is it that __________?* You can fill in the blank, but for many, it is the bigger house, the fancier car, the boat that has all your friends wanting to join you for the weekend. It could be a job position that you know you have earned. It can be many *this* or *thats*, but many times it comes down to possessions and/or power.

"If you wish to be complete," Jesus said, "go and sell your possessions and give to the poor, and you will have treasure in heaven"; and oh, By The Way, "Come, follow Me."[8]

If you are familiar with the account, you know what happens next, and we have a sense of empathy for the *do-gooder*. When he heard this, you could say his heart sank in a sea of unwillingness, and "he went away grieving; for he was one who owned much property" (v. 22). You could say his balance sheet had rewarded him handsomely but left him unbalanced spiritually and left behind in his goal to obtain eternal life, which was his opening dialogue and question to know what he should, could, or would do.

By The Way. Jesus said to His disciples, to those who chose to follow Him when He said, "Come, follow me," "You know the way," for "I am the Way, the Truth and the Life."[9] So, there it is! *By The Way* is a person. *The Way* is Jesus. Following Him in His footsteps, going where He leads, and never being left behind.

FINDING THE UNIMAGINABLE

We may go through life knowing but never expecting, and then it comes, and something we are never sufficiently trained for is before us to accept and champion in a way we know is not from us, and we find we are like Him, Jesus our Lord.

During our lifetimes, many of us have been surprised by what we have found unexpectedly, and if not jumping for joy, at least a broad smile has come across our faces. I remember one time I was just walking along during a lunch break at work and found twenty dollars that had blown into the weeds with no one around to question a loss. I can't remember exactly, as it was many years ago, but I'm pretty sure it was a timely discovery at a time of need. There have been so many similar occasions (not just finding money) that have left me sure that there are angels watching over me, providing unexpectedly, keeping me out of trouble, even saving me from disaster. The orchestra of life is playing, and the maestro is conducting a symphony blended with choice instruments that alone cannot make the magnificent music that astounds even the most seasoned listeners. We can search the scores written, and it is hard to imagine how such notes can be combined in totally different ways to achieve such glorious sound that is more than just pleasing to hear. The more we become acquainted with such productions, the more we have to be careful not to take these great compositions for granted.

Life plays out that way, and we find ourselves trying to find where we fit into this grand scene of God's glory, making sure the right notes are being played. That unimaginable does come unexpectedly at times to help tune our part, and we tip a nod to the Maestro in recognition of the intervention.

The irony is that the unimaginable has found us. It is a find that simply *landed in our laps*, which is an old expression worth revitalizing. You have experienced it, and more than once, I'm sure, trying so hard for something—a possession you desire, an achievement that has been evasive, and then you just let go, knowing that on your own it just won't happen. Your trust is no longer in what you can do, and maybe you just give up on the dream.

What happens next in your experience? This is where you write your story, and I estimate that the number of pages may be surprising. We have a Father who gives good gifts and one most important that enables us to know Him. We know how to give good gifts to our children, even when they don't ask. How much more, we are told, will our heavenly Father give the Holy Spirit if we ask? That is truly unimaginable, but we find that we are indwelled with His presence, alive in us, revealing His nature and character such that it is manifested in our lives to be seen and experienced by others. The unseen has been seen, the unheard has been heard, and life takes on a dimension that is beyond understanding. Simply unimaginable.

There is a caveat here, a warning that whosoever believeth in him should not perish but have eternal life. *Why a warning?* —will surely be asked. It is in the believing that leads to discipleship, a follower. And Jesus says to such, "Whoever wants to be my disciple must deny themselves and take up their cross and follow me. For whoever wants to save their life will lose it, but whoever loses their life for me will find it. What good will it be for someone to gain the whole world, yet forfeit their soul? Or what can anyone give in exchange for their soul?"[10]

Offer the whole world to someone, especially the deprived; who would not accept such an offer? Who does not try and live as long as possible, saving their lives from trouble and an end they do not desire? There is a life difference being alluded to here. A difference in life's perspective. But more than a perspective, a belief. Do we walk through life by faith or by sight? Some have said, if I see it I will believe it—I think they were from Oklahoma. *Seeing is believing* is another axiom professed by those that would still exclaim, *I can't believe it. I see it, but I can't believe it.*

Peter wrote, "Though you have not seen Him, you love Him and even though you do not see Him now, you believe in Him and are filled with an inexpressible and glorious joy for you are receiving the goal of your faith the salvation of your souls."[11]

The unimaginable has been found, and the glory of the Lord is declared as we walk with Him. Finding the unimaginable is not so hard when we no longer trust in ourselves and trust in the One who will grant us the unimaginable. It is no longer a surprise finding but an amazing grace that showers us in blessings that bring unimaginable beauty to our lives. "Seek ye first His kingdom and His righteousness and all of these things will be added unto you."[12]

8

HEARING IS SEEKING

You hear the brook and oh, how soothing and relaxing. You hunt for the sound you hear. It is hard to explain, but when you find it and just stare mesmerized, it is a look that, without the sound, would be empty of the beauty discovered.

You may have heard the expression, "You hear what you want to hear." There are probably a thousand and one circumstances that led to that expressed conviction. The conclusion is that the hearing is woven in with our perceptions and formulates a conceived notion, true or not.

There is an axiom of communication that, without listening, one cannot hear. Sound may be heard, but without listening, there is no communication; nothing is really heard and processed into knowing what was said.

It stands to reason, then, if anything is heard and therefore processed, one has been listening and actually seeking to know what is being said. We seek to know by hearing.

Did you know that you also can hear by seeing and processing through sight? OK, you are probably smiling at this and saying, *Duh, it's called reading.* But the seeing I'm referring to goes much deeper than sight. Think of the expression, *I can see that now;* you aren't really looking at anything. Something has processed in your mind that makes sense, and you have come to acknowledge what you believe—what you believe is truth. The psalmist wrote, "Open my eyes, that I may behold wonderful things from Your law."[13] The beholding is not in the seeing; it is in the knowing from a seeking that is before the Lord.

Most spiritual things are not seen but heard. There are visions, but they are usually selected, being designated to a person, time, and place. Spiritually, hearing can take place anywhere at any time, moving like the wind—like the wind of the Spirit, sharing the voice of God. That notwithstanding, a vision, too, can be unexpected and surprising, as we know in scripture, but if we ask around for who has had a vision from God, most likely there will be very few, if any, in response. But ask who has ever heard the voice of God, and an orchestra of responses will come from believers, young and old. It is by the power of the Holy Spirit that we hear spiritual things that lead us as children of God. Paul wrote, "For all who are being led by the Spirit of God, these are sons and daughters of God."[14] It is possible to be led blindly, as some say, but it is impossible to be led without hearing. It is a privileged indwelling that opens our ears to spiritual things. Paul also wrote, "Blessed be the God and Father of our Lord Jesus Christ, who has blessed us with every spiritual blessing in the heavenly places in Christ."[15] Further writing, he shares, "In Him, you also, after listening to the message of truth, the gospel of your salvation—having also believed, you were sealed in Him with the Holy Spirit of promise, who is given as a pledge of our inheritance, with a view to the redemption of God's own possession, to the praise of His glory."[16]

Listening and hearing, seeking truths that define our purpose, our place with our Lord and others, is an inherent purpose of God in everyone. Some receive and believe in the truths, others reject them, but the nature of all mankind is to hear, seeking truths of the what, where, why, and how that define them.

God has placed a voice in the seeking. John recorded the words of our Lord, writing, "My sheep hear My voice, and I know them, and they follow Me."[17] Luke wrote in his Gospel, "In the high priesthood of Annas and Caiaphas, the word of God came to John, the son of Zacharias, in the wilderness. . . . as it is written in the book of the words of Isaiah the prophet, 'The voice of one crying in the wilderness, make ready the way of the Lord, make His paths straight.'"[18] Daniel wrote, "While the word was in the king's mouth, a voice came from heaven."[19] It is clear the unheard can be heard, which is foolishness to the carnal man, the unbeliever, but is the power of God to the believer. The spiritually dead seldom seek or hear God's voice, but I am convinced that they all come to a crossroads where opportunity lies to open the deaf ears and hear the voice of God. Jeremiah records a particular crossroads exclaimed by the Lord: "Stand at the crossroads and look and ask for the ancient paths, where the good way is and walk in it."[20] For those who choose rightly, death no longer has a hold on them. John records words spoken by Jesus: "Truly, truly, I say to you, an hour is coming and now is, when the dead will hear the voice of the Son of God, and those who hear will live."[21]

Hearing is seeking. To be clear, a hearing's foundation is seeking with a purpose. To demonstrate this woven tapestry of senses and motive, the account of Solomon's wisdom presents this nature vividly. Recorded in 1 Kings, it states that "Men came from all peoples to hear the wisdom of Solomon, from all the kings of the earth who had heard of his wisdom."[22]

Spiritually, hearing is seeking life itself—life everlasting. The word of the Lord endures forever; be prepared to hear the word of the Lord and seek to hear and hear to seek. We find in Peter's epistle such a state of preparation: "Therefore, prepare your minds for action, keep sober in spirit, fix your hope completely on the grace to be brought to you at the revelation of Jesus Christ."[23]

Have you heard to seek and sought to hear? It is the thread that weaves itself into a kingdom tapestry on earth, leading to heaven's gate, and you are no longer left with or limited to just five senses that allow you to explore who you really are.

9

LOVE WORTH FINDING

And they crowded at the seashore because His teaching reached their hearts, and they felt a love never experienced before from an unknown friend.

The previous chapter noted a seeking that, I believe, is inherent to all mankind, and purpose and motives are the engine that moves us on a path to reach our goal(s). Have you ever heard the expression, *Was it really worth it?* Many times, we set out to achieve or gain something, and when we finally reach our plateau, we find some disappointment waiting at the door—or at least a letdown because it wasn't all that we thought it would be. The world of psychoanalysis would say this is to be expected and, in many ways, can be prepared for to minimize the dissonance it brings in planning new horizons.

What is it that we typically set our minds on? Things we feel will bring happiness and security and a life without worry? Financial security and possessions that bring pleasure? Someone to share with and who agrees with us . . . most of the time? I am hoping that the discussion opens your hearts and minds to what really is your aim, the target that is out there that is your focus. I'm sure there is much more than what I have listed, but I think we can categorize them into one of two thoughts on how to achieve those virtuous goals: setting our minds on things that are above or setting our minds on things that are on earth. Happiness, security, and no worries would be an accurate assessment for any *desirable* journey through life, both for those who reject focusing on the things above and for those who know where the source for that achievement is found—those who believe in God above, His Son, and the Holy Spirit, a Trinity of love that was expressed in a monumental sacrifice for His family to live in such a joyous journey. The new self is what leaves worries behind and brings the security and joy in life that is always and forever. Solomon wrote, "But whoever listens to me will live securely and will be at ease from the dread of evil."[24] Paul wrote to the church in Colossae, "Set your minds on the things that are above, not on the things that are on earth. For you have died, and your life is hidden with Christ in God. When Christ, who is our life, is revealed, then you also will be revealed with Him in Glory."[25]

Colossae was what is today Turkey, and Paul, in his letter, refuted the many lies that were being purported as truths: hollow and deceptive philosophies that afforded old ways, and wrong ways that always result in pain and suffering, leading to despair rather than desires found in fruitful life. Pain and suffering come to all who have ever walked on this earth, but the difference is in the results of endurance and overcoming in victory rather than falling in defeat. The emptiness of mere human philosophy simply cannot be seen by many seeking ways that seem right. Paul writes, "See to it that no one takes you captive through philosophy and empty deception, according to the tradition of men, according to the elementary principles of the world, rather than according to Christ."[26] Arguably, this is in reference to heresy in the church regarding faith beliefs, but it is not too far of a stretch to include worldly ways that steal hearts and minds from truth.

I have to interject here with a simple but serious caution: don't buy the lie! There is one evil upon evil that makes bad look good and good look bad. A changing of the guard of conceptions and perceptions that can fool anyone if not on guard, standing firm in strength that is given when asked for. From the beginning, this strategy of deceitfulness has been the bedrock of failures that can reap havoc for a lifetime and even generations to come, and when the reality of truth strikes, it is too late; the damage has been done.

So how do we guard against these travesties that can devour us to the core? Well, Paul didn't leave the church folks wondering or worrying about what to do, how to be prepared against evil onslaughts. He continued in his writing,

Therefore if you have been raised up with Christ [a pretty good upbringing], keep seeking the things above, where Christ is, seated at the right hand of God. Set your mind on the things above, not on things that are on earth. For you have died and your life is hidden with Christ in God. When Christ, who is our life, is revealed, then you also will be revealed with Him in glory. Therefore consider the members of your earthly body as dead to immorality, impurity, passion, evil desire, and greed, which amounts to idolatry. For it is because of these things that the wrath of God will come upon the sons of disobedience, and in them you also once walked, when you were living in them. But now you also, put them all aside; anger, wrath,

> *malice, slander, and abusive speech from your mouth. Do not lie to one another, since you laid aside the old self with its evil practices, and have put on the new self who is being renewed to a true knowledge according to the image of the One who created him. (Col. 3:1-10)*

Being holy and beloved, we have,

> *. . . put on a heart of compassion, kindness, humility, gentleness, and patience; bearing with one another, and forgiving each other, whoever has a complaint against anyone; just as the Lord forgave you, so also should you. Beyond all these things put on love, which is the perfect bond of unity. Let the peace of Christ rule in your hearts, to which indeed you were called in one body; and be thankful. Let the word of Christ richly dwell within you, with all wisdom teaching and admonishing one another with psalms and hymns and spiritual songs, singing with thankfulness in*

> *your hearts to God. Whatever you do in word or deed, do all in the name of the Lord Jesus, giving thanks through Him to God the Father. (Col. 3:12-17)*

Someone once said, *What can you say when all has been said?* That is how I feel about what more is needed to be said that has already been said in this succinct and pragmatic instruction to the church in Colossae. It pronounces a transformation that has been made, screaming out differences that make the difference we all yearn for in our communities, our country, our world, our church. And what is the preponderance of truth? Love, which is the basic ingredient and motive for such a transformation to be made visible. A love worth finding. Peter, in writing one of his epistles, exhorts the same saintly character that makes the difference: "For this very reason, make every effort to add to your faith, goodness, and to goodness, knowledge and to knowledge, self-control, and to self-control, perseverance and to perseverance, godliness and to godliness, brotherly kindness, and to brotherly kindness, love, for if you possess these qualities in increasing measure they will keep you from becoming ineffective and unproductive in the true knowledge of our Lord Jesus Christ."[27]

Notice the progression in goodness to love. It is unmistakable that everything adds to and combines while ending in love. We are dearly beloved children of God such that we can live a life of love.

To the church in Ephesus, it was written, "Be imitators [followers from the original Greek] of God therefore, as dearly beloved children; and live a life of love, just as Christ loved us and gave Himself up as a fragrant offering and sacrifice to God."[28]

A love worth finding: the Love of God. A love worth living: a fragrant offering and sacrifice to God. Paul again writes, "Therefore I urge you brethren to offer your bodies as a living sacrifice, holy and pleasing to God—this is your true and proper worship."[29]

A love worth finding. A love that is ours in Christ that makes the difference for many in life or death. God sets before us that way of life and the way of death. Choosing life, well, who would choose otherwise?

10

VICTORY AT SEE

Hey, I'm floating in the sea, and then there is the unseen behind me, holding me up.

Armies always measure the battle, judging the size of enemy forces, the strength of the armament, and critical aspects that can determine the outcome in victory or defeat. Spies are sent out and even planted to gain valuable information to secure advantage over the opponent. And then there is the unknown, the unseen that determines the significance of the risk that the planning and assessments may well fall short of in what is needed for victory. Sometimes that risk seems too great to send armies into battle, which leads to defeat from simply fearing the odds.

We see in biblical accounts where battles are not fought alone by man and where the Lord exclaims the battle is His. Writings in Chronicles share where Jahaziel, a Levitical priest, tells all Judah and the inhabitants of Jerusalem and King Jehoshaphat that the ensuing battle against the Ammonites and Moabites who are coming to drive them out of the land God has given them is not their battle but God's.

Another account opens eyes to see the unseen for courage to go into battle, knowing the victory is won. A writer in the book of Kings presents a plot by the Arameans, who were warring against Israel, to capture Elisha. Elisha's servant knows the city is encircled by invaders and shares his concern about what to do:

> *Now the attendant of the man of God had risen early and gone out, behold, an army with horses and chariots was circling the city. And his servant said to him, "Alas, my master! What shall we do?" So, he answered, "Do not fear, for those who are with us are more than those who are with them." Then Elisha prayed and said, "O Lord, I pray, open his eyes that he may see." And the Lord opened the servant's eyes and he saw; and behold, the mountain was full of horses and chariots of fire all around Elisha. (2 Kings 6:15-17)*

It may be that Elisha and his servant were the only ones that saw the company of warriors. We can be sure that the enemies' army could not see them, or they simply would have fled the city. So, when eyes are opened by the Lord, what is seen is the unseen, and a perceived defeat becomes victory simply by seeing. This is not for the faint of faith, for only by faith can eyes be opened to the unseen, and legions upon legions of angels accompany the Lord and those to whom He sends them. But even without visually seeing, we can be sure of the angelic accompaniment because we have heard, and hearing, we have found, is seeking *victory at see*.

11

SURVIVAL OF THE UNFITTEST

Tired of the journey and feel like quitting?
You can rest in Him, all you who are weary
and burdened; He will give you rest.

I believe we have all experienced a letdown a time or two, and we can go back to early childhood and remember when we were not chosen until the very last, or close to it, to be part of a selected team of some sort. And for us runners who may have struggled to finish a race, maybe at times wanting to give up, the sight of the finish line is better than a boost of Red Bull. Even though chosen last or struggling to finish, it is always encouraging knowing you were chosen and knowing you crossed the finish line.

The difference between *victory* and *defeat* is found in the heart, and true victory, I am confident, can be found when we are dead last—or should I say, *dead at last*. The greatest victory ever recorded for mankind was what the world saw as a defeat—one seen most unfit to claim who He was. Called a blasphemer and worthy only of torture and death. Shunned by many, and those who were on His side even walked away.

How does one survive the jaws of defeat? How do you climb out from rock-bottom? Who is it that is there to encourage you when you are exhausted, to lift you up when you are most feeble? Well, there is a change, a transformation that can take place when the odds of the world have trampled you down, and you are most vulnerable. A change not to finally bury you in defeat but that makes you vulnerable to finding a victory that could not come otherwise.

Isaiah penned such, finding victory in the midst of defeat in one of Israel's darkest hours that would become one of their brightest shining moments, writing,

> The wilderness and the desert will be glad, and the Arabah will rejoice and blossom; like the crocus it will blossom profusely and rejoice with rejoicing and shout of joy. The glory of Lebanon will be given to it, the majesty of Carmel and Sharon. They will see the glory of the Lord, the majesty of God. Encourage the exhausted, and strengthen the feeble. Say to those with anxious heart, take courage, fear not. Behold, your God will come with vengeance; the recompense of God will come, but He will save you. Then the eyes of the blind will be opened and the ears of the deaf will be unstopped. Then the lame will leap like a deer, and the tongue of the mute will shout for

> joy. For waters will break forth in the wilderness and streams in the Arabah. The scorched land will become a pool and the thirsty ground springs of water; in the haunt of jackals, its resting place, grass becomes reeds and rushes. A highway will be there, a roadway, and it will be called the Highway of Holiness. The unclean will not travel on it, but it will be for him who walks that way, and fools will not wander on it. No lion will be there, nor will any vicious beast go up on it; these will not be found there. But the redeemed will walk there, and the ransomed of the Lord will return and come with joyful shouting to Zion, with everlasting joy upon their heads. They will find gladness and joy, and sorrow and sighing will flee away. (Isa. 35:1-10)

What can we take away from this enlightenment? What can sink into our hearts, listening and absorbing the meaning of the truths shared in prophecy and historical fact? I believe it is a message of three defining characteristics of our Lord Jesus: forgiveness, mercy, and grace. Identifying and believing that person and those qualities of life, life everlasting, breeds perseverance, a never-give-up attitude character trait that knows the un-fittest survival is promised and assured. Not only survival in the least but survival in the most glorious joy everlasting and gladness.

I am convinced that the Lord never asks us to be successful according to the world and its ways but to be faithful to Him always. The successes in the world may or may not come. My experience is that they do if we faithfully walk with the Lord, for "His divine power has given us everything we need in life and godliness through our knowledge of Him who has called us by His own glory and goodness."[30] The personal words of our Lord promise that our heavenly Father knows what we need, and if we seek first His kingdom and His righteousness, all of what we need will be given to us, unworthy as we are. How can we deserve all that He has given us and all that He will continue to give us to survive and survive as champions of the faith?

KNOWING YOU

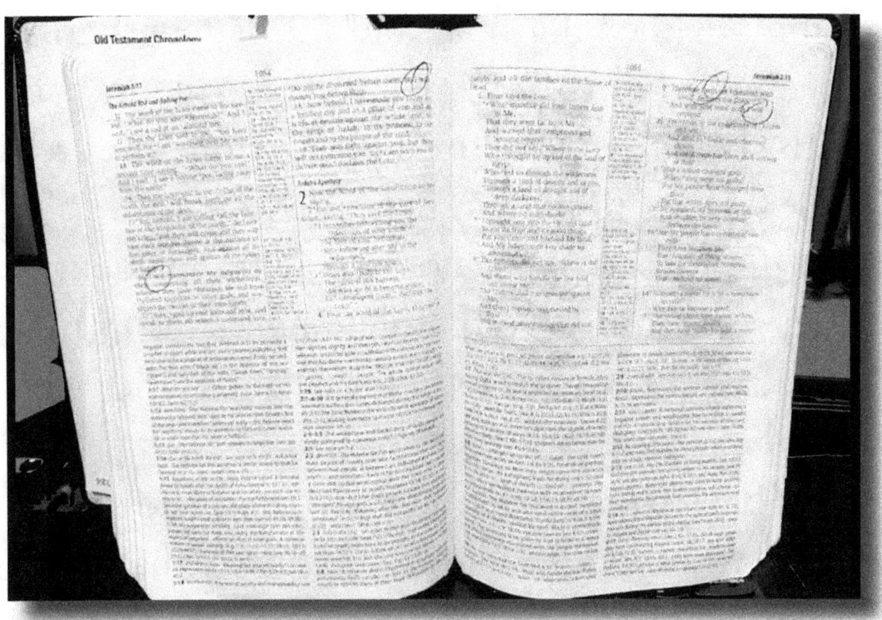

These pages are marked forever as a covenant—not in a book that can get left behind but upon hearts of those who know Me, says the Lord. "'This is the covenant I will make with the house of Israel after that time,' declares the Lord. 'I will put my law within them and on their hearts I will write it. I will be their God and they will be My people'" (Jer. 31:33).

We have come to the last chapter in this section of what has hopefully brought you closer to the Lord, knowing not just about Him but knowing Him and intimately sharing time with Him, growing and maturing in your faith, being fruit falling not far from the tree. True, we are to remain as branches, but we also venture out to be recognized with an identity that is a shining light before men that they may see our good works and glorify our Father who is in heaven.

That's it, a proven identity that shows you know who you are. I am convinced that apart from truly knowing Christ, we can never know ourselves—who we truly are. You've heard the expression, *Knowing you inside and out.* That holds true for us as well in knowing ourselves.

But how can we come to know God, even what some would say knowing His deep secrets? Henry Blackaby wrote in *Experiencing God* that by reading the Bible, the Word of God, by being faithful in prayer, by being in fellowship, and by the circumstances succinctly orchestrated by God, we can know Him.[31] Those four criteria can reach a cosmic collision that transpires at the cross: a collision of justice and grace. We recognize who He is and realize who we are, and from that a union is formed that opens the floodgates of a relationship that ushers in wisdom, knowledge, and understanding, never before grasped because of limitations that held us captive, not unlike the experiences that beheld His chosen people of old.

Some years ago, I had just graduated with my master's in Christian studies, and we had made a trip to Washington, D.C., to explore all the historical monuments and places of government. My walk along the mall to take in all of the Washington Monument was interrupted by a homeless man looking for help, simply asking, "Do you have a dollar?" Out of me, in an unexpected way, I'm sure, exploded the question, "Do you love Jesus?" He responded, "I do not know the man." His name was Robert, and at the time I am writing this, I am searching my mind to remember his last name, as I inquired. I may have it written down somewhere because, over the years, I continued to pray for him. Though not important here, what was important was that I stopped and spent time telling him about our Lord. Now, so that you know and have a picture of this encounter, my wife was with me and seemed a bit anxious to move on and had separated herself some distance from us but was waiting; I wasn't in a hurry and was going to spend as much time as Robert would allow. My memory of the ending was that at the time, though I could tell he accepted much of what I told him, he was not ready to receive Jesus as his Savior, and he ended by asking, "But do you have a dollar?" Unfortunately (or fortunately), I did not have any cash with me, and by now my wife was sufficiently far off to where I could not ask her to help, and I just said that what I shared with him was more valuable than what money could provide for him.

As the years would pass, I had a genuine feeling that Robert came to know the Lord and received him as his Savior. I don't have any proof, but you may know how sometimes revelation comes in mysterious ways, and hope does not disappoint you.

Now here's the other side of the story before you start thinking, *What a nice testimony.* Looking and thinking back, Robert (and now, I'm pretty sure his last name was Walker) may well have known Jesus and had an intimate relationship with Him. You may be a seasoned Christian reading this, and you will know the account of Simon Peter standing outside the court of the high priest when he denied knowing Jesus three times. Peter certainly had a personal, intimate relationship with Jesus and had been with Him, and when asked previously by Jesus, "But who do you say that I am?" he answered, "You are the Christ, the Son of the Living God" (Matt. 16:16). Peter certainly knew Jesus well but denied knowing Him. Could Robert have known Jesus and known Him well? I believe he surely could have. Though he appeared and acted homeless, needing to ask for handouts, faith in Jesus and knowing Him has no economic barriers. Robert may very well have been thinking, *What, if anything, does this White boy, walking along the Mall of Washington, D.C., looking like he is on a vacation, know, and what can he tell me about*

Jesus? We often don't know the spiritual reality of circumstances the Lord creates in our paths, which I believe is far more important to know than the visible reality before us. Jesus Himself may have posed the question, "But who do you say that I am?" Do you really know Me, or do you just know about Me from what you have read and have been told? The deep intimacy of a personal relationship, yet not alone and in needed fellowship with others in a holistic body that serves our Lord, is what separates ones who say they know from ones who yield to a Master—obedient to His very beckoning.

His honesty in response to the question (*Do you love Jesus?*) opened a door I believe we were at, waiting for an unknown opportunity that had been orchestrated by our Lord—a heart seeking with the mind unaware that it would be reminded of truths that reveal the pathway to new horizons and rebirth. I feel we both took the challenge and walked further along that path into the open arms of a Father that welcomes us to a celebration that spills into the streets that lead many astray.

The Bible in its entirety is a revelation of God, who He is, and how, in His sovereignty, the plan to claim all His creation unfolds before us, for it is rightly His.

Ecclesiastes in the Old Testament may be a book that is infrequently read compared to others, but it reveals one who is wisest in life, and it challenges readers, anticipating many of the problems facing a young life of today, and brings to solution the one and only key—the realization of the Lord Jesus Christ in every relationship of life.[32]

The writings of David, who is exclaimed as having a heart after God, disclose an intimacy that allows us to "get close" in our own relationship and begin to know the God who made us. I could rewrite the entire book of Psalms so that could be captured, but I will just refer to some of the verses to incite that endeavor.

> *For in the hand of the Lord there is a cup, and the wine is red; it is full of mixture; and he poureth out of the same: but the dregs thereof, all the*

> *wicked of the earth shall wring them out, and drink them. (Ps. 75:8)*

I find it interesting relating Old Testament writings with the threaded tapestry of New Testament writings, and the psalm above I will compliment with a citing Oswald Chambers makes regarding Paul's writing to the church in Rome: "All things are permitted by God, but all things are not appointed by God, they appoint themselves; but God's order abides, and if I maintain my relationship to Him He will make everything that happens work for my good. God on the one hand, myself on the other, and the rush of the haphazard in between will work toward the best."[33]

One thing that is revealed as we read through the Bible is the unseen world that has rulers and majesties and supernatural beings, we know little about but that are not of God. We find that man at his own peril was able to communicate with them in the world, and finding being possessed by them is a reality. Our God does not take kindly to such instances, and we find many times His interceding leads to an undesirable end—some of which is unexplainable. The only explanation comes through a personal knowledge and trust of God through Jesus Christ. Any philosophy or thinking that finds its way into the minds of men will always leave one searching for understanding.

Life gives us sufficient reason to seek that personal knowledge and relationship, to know the truths behind the perplexing. Our Lord's promise is that "you will know the truth, and the truth will set you free."[34] When you are freed from the anxiety of the world, you find a peace that has always been at your door. It is not a peace that comes from understanding but a peace we do know that is beyond our comprehension. Faith is trust that we have in God, whose ways are far above any that we know of our own but whose character we do know. I will list many of those traits throughout this last chapter (of Part 1) so that we can direct our minds to reflect on just who this, our Lord, is. At the least we will attest that He is a God of honor. We cannot know Him by human reasoning, though that is how we most often approach Him when questioning the curves thrown at us in life. The true revelation of Him is through the Holy Spirit freely given once Christ Himself is received and believed through faith. A whole new world opens up in front of us, and scales come off our eyes, and we begin to hear a still, small voice we were deaf to prior to accepting His invitation to come and follow Him. At this point He begins the molding process, like hands on clay, and shapes us in a way that looks like Him in character and purpose. It's a heart massage that stirs the blood flow like never before, and we all know that getting more blood to the brain can remove the dizziness that cripples us when we need to be most vibrant in our thinking.

This molding (as many of you can attest) takes us through some very unpleasant experiences in our life journey. Sometimes it leaves us in a state of status quo with little change in our daily routines. We can go through times when nothing much is noticed about us, there are no banners and no sounding trumpets, but slowly and surely the character of Christ begins to be seen. The seal of a family likeness to Jesus Christ becomes apparent to those around us, and like His early disciples, folks note, *they have been with Jesus!*

The details of our life begin to overflow in the manifestation of One living in us, following in footsteps along a path that is the right way. You've heard the expression, "He is following in his father's footsteps," which simply designates the likeness of father and son in purpose and pursuit. It is not that we take over the duty, but in likeness we become part of the harvest of God that He, in advance, is already working, and the fruit of the Spirit is made ready in our lives. We experience with others a love that defies the world's definitions, a joy that is not stagnant but overflowing, a peace that transcends understanding, surprising patience that is present even in affliction, a kindness that returns to our very doorstep, a goodness that gets credited to us as righteousness, faithfulness that seeks first the kingdom of God and His righteousness, gentleness that soothes a roaring lion, and self-control when all odds are against us. How can it be that these can be ours but with the Lord in us?

John shares in his Gospel the words of our Lord Jesus that bring this to the test of reality: "I am the vine, you are the branches; he who abides in Me and I in him, he bears much fruit, for apart from Me you can do nothing."[35] It is the discipline of the Lord that enables us to be fruitful, carrying His light through dark places. A true love always disciplines the heart so that all things find their roots in treasure found only in the heavenly realms, a first love that began all things—God demonstrating His own love toward us even when we were walking alone in our own way. It is His nature, His being. It is the way He is. It is who He is. And when we have gained His nature, we can perceive all things in the light He brings. He can be who He is in us as we rid ourselves of the old nature. It is truly as Jesus says, a rebirth in the Spirit of God that makes all things new. What we often lack when we are walking in our own way, trying to solve many of life's challenges, is our Lord's perspective. We see things in the light we have turned on in our rooms rather than in the light that shines in our hearts, and we wonder why the light is flickering and needs replacing.

We question our perspectives in the light of what we know, and many times we compare ourselves with others to justify conjecture. Peter (many of us are compared with his nature), when our Lord signified in what kind of death he would glorify God, said to him, "Follow Me!"[36] The closeness Peter had with the other disciples and particularly John must have had him wondering about their fate as he asked, "And what about this man?"[37]—directing his attention to the Apostle John. Jesus' response was one that rings true for all followers and for all ages: "Jesus said to him, 'If I want him to remain until I come, what is that to you? You follow Me!'"[38]

This looking at ourselves in comparison to others can leave us empty of what the Lord intends for us. He does not ask us to keep up with the Joneses or to even be successful in the world's ways. He asks us to remain faithful and follow Him and not worry about what He has made ready for others. Don't get me wrong. We are fellow workers of God. We are His body, and we are to be in concert, helping one another to accomplish His will, and it matters that we recognize how our part of the body fits with the others. Our faithfulness is the bedrock of how we think and act, and it is the assurance of things hoped for and the conviction of things not seen, so it transcends differences that complicate things in life and relationships in and outside of His body. We are to make the concerns of God our concerns, and our perspectives will line up in holiness, the holiness of God. We begin to get it right more than wrong, regardless of circumstances. God and His will is our focus, and the myriads of audiences is dimed in His presence as we strive to please Him in sacrifice. Our Lord, worthy of His rightful place, sees Himself as Master, our Master in ownership. We bring Him to bear as Healer, Savior, and Sanctifier. We experience that in relationship, and His truths have us confiding in one as Master. Our obedience is the outcome of recognizing who He is and realizing who we are (I have said this before).[39]

The test of truly knowing God is the knowledge of His character and doing His will. John wrote in his Epistle,

> *By this we know that we have come to know Him, if we keep His commandments. The one who says, "I have come to know Him," and does not keep His commandments, is a liar, and the truth is not in him; but whoever keeps His word, in the love of God has truly been perfected. By this we know that we are in Him; the one who says he abides in Him ought himself to walk in the same manner as He walked. (1 John 2:3-6)*

It is not God's promise we need, though you cannot separate the promises from the person; it is God Himself. Not just knowing what He does for us but knowing who He is. We may not always know what He is doing in and through us, but we come to know Him, and in faith our confidence is built up in a Person whose character we know gives illumination perfectly at the right time. The psalmist wrote,

> *Whom have I in heaven but You? And besides you, I desire nothing on earth. My flesh and my heart may fail, but God is the strength of my heart and my portion forever. For, behold, those who are far from you will perish; You have destroyed all those who are unfaithful to You. But as for me, the nearness of God is my good; I have made the Lord God my refuge, that I may tell of all Your works. (Ps. 73:25-28)*

Inseparable is what comes to my mind. He in us and us in Him. The identity that announces it's not about me. A humility found and founded in the holiness of God. "Let your light shine," Jesus says, "before men in such a way that they may see your good works and glorify your Father who is in heaven."[40] Man's earthly/worldly desire is to glory in himself; what he has done is the announcement, and he revels in the accolades that acclaim a glorification that fades from the very moment it is afforded. But the righteous in godly humility stand ready to receive nothing except that the Father Himself is praised, honored, and glorified.

Producing wealth is the result of the abiding that is spiritually *mano a mano*. Riches not of the earth but of heaven. Moses wrote, "Remember the Lord your God for it is He who gives you the ability to produce wealth and so confirms His covenant which He swore to your fathers, as it is today" (Deut. 8:18). Spiritual enablement, as we see also in the words *priest* and *prophet*, Zechariah penned from an angel speaking words of the Lord: "This is the word of the Lord to Zerubbabel saying, Not by might, nor by power, but by My Spirit, says the Lord of hosts."[41] The completion of the second building of the temple in Jerusalem would be glorious, and we are reminded, as was Zerubbabel, that our accomplishments find their roots in an ability that is beyond us, and the rightful recipient of the glory that comes resides above the earthly realm.

I'm a runner and have run many marathons, half marathons, 10ks, and 5ks and have many podium finishes, but I am reminded that with all the training I do, there is something more that allows me to enjoy the sport, something more that gives me strength, something more that gives me wings like eagles, and I am able to run without growing wearing or tired—at least during the race. It is somewhat different the day after finishing a marathon at seventy-three years old. The pain I feel is actually benefiting my body, building up the muscles to be even stronger, and in the recouperation there resides an untold strength from the covering of prayer from beginning to end that is the ointment that soothes the weary muscles and bones. I can see that in many of the painful episodes we experience in life. Staying close, waiting on the Lord, promises to renew our strength, emerging stronger.

Note that running is a sport that singles out the performance of the individual for the most part when competing. I say *for the most part* because for the novice or even the intermediary, this is true. But for the elite or professional, there are pacers that draw out more than runners can do by themselves. We develop friendships that, in similar ways, (should) lead us to a deeper, better knowledge of God. It is how the body of Christ functions. Our dependence remains on God but is coupled by the relationship in friendship, and we are able to be more than we could be by ourselves. This is true as well for fruitful marriages. Going through life alone may bring satisfaction, but we would never reach our potential in the purpose of God without others He has led us to.

The way God has made us always has us working in concert with the seen and unseen. Everyone has a given intelligence, but apart from the Lord, it is just a moral ascent. Those of us who have received Christ as our Savior also have a spontaneous originality of the Holy Spirit and a constant communion with God, knowing The Way, The Truth, and The Life. A word or scripture will be brought to mind just at the right time and right place, and there is an epiphany—an aha moment—that steers us rightly, and our hearts well up in praise and thanksgiving. Life in its fullness begins to be experienced in a realm that transcends the seen in the unseen. The spiritual realm is just as real as the physical earthly realm. It is the Holy Spirit who develops the deep, deep love that only knowing God can usher in; you know what is beyond knowing. We position ourselves walking through life on bended knees and reflect as Paul, in writing to the church goers in Ephesus,

For this reason I bow my knees before the Father, from whom every family in heaven and on earth derives its name, that He would grant you, according to the riches of His glory, to be strengthened with power through His Spirit in the inner man, so that Christ may dwell in your hearts through faith; and that you, being rooted and grounded in love, may be able to comprehend with all the saints what is the breadth and length and height and depth, and to know the love of Christ which surpasses knowledge, that you may be filled up to all the fullness of God. Now to Him who is able to do far more abundantly beyond all that we ask or think, according to the power that works within us, to Him be the glory in the church and in Christ Jesus to all generations forever and ever. Amen. (Eph. 3:14-21)

The kingdom of God is within us here on earth. We really don't have to wait to meet Him, but oh, what a day when we see Him face to face! There will come a day when the kingdom of God will be outside as well as inside. We and our Lord's message are one. We become living billboards, and as we mature, we add lights so that we can be read in the dark. There is a way of holiness that is broadcasted with every step we take, and it is an enlightenment that begins with the holiness of God. "Be holy for I am holy" were His words through the prophet Habakuk and were repeated by Peter in his Epistle: "But like the Holy One who called you, be holy yourselves also in all your behavior; because it is written, 'YOU SHALL BE HOLY, FOR I AM HOLY.'"[42]

Our Father is glorified in the holiness of His saints, and we see that in a Holy vine. Branches sprout out the same holiness from the source, and the essential nature is not only found in the branches but also in the fruit that it bears. John writes in his Gospel account of the very words spoken by our Lord Jesus: "My Father is glorified by this, that you bear much fruit, and so prove to be my disciples."[43]

It is essential to understand the holiness of God that I believe precedes everything that He asks of us. Our Lord always goes before us, preparing our hearts and minds for the tasks needing to be accomplished. We see that in the lives of two whom I will mention, Moses and Joshua. Interestingly it was Joshua who succeeded Moses in leadership, and their preparation was similar regarding their knowing Who it was that was calling, guiding, and equipping them for work that was to be done. Moses first was called to lead God's people out of Egyptian bondage to a land He was giving them. But He would not enter that land; it was Joshua who had that honor in leading Israel into the land of "milk and honey." But what was the similarity in God's revealing Himself?

Moses would be led to the far side of the wilderness, where Horeb, the mountain of God, was located. Behold, he would find a "burning bush" that would not be extinguished and, as he approached it, was a strange sight to him. (I'm sure any one of us would be overcome with curiosity). God called to him by name from within the bush, and Moses responded, "Here I am."[44] The Lord cautioned him to not come any closer and to remove his sandals, for he was standing on holy ground. Now this was ground that was pretty much rocky, desert ground on the Sinai Peninsula and was not a place you would (in those days) choose for a relaxing vacation. You might say it was inhabited by unholy creatures you would find in that type of environment. So what would make such ground so desirable, so precious, so different? There is only one explanation, and that is *the presence of God and His holiness, and the Lord always requires this to be known and revered.* God tells Moses that He has seen the misery from the oppression of His people in Egypt and heard their crying, and being concerned, He has come down to rescue them, and He is sending Moses to bring them out.

Leaping forward to when Israel had just entered the Promised Land under Joshua's leadership that had been passed on by Moses under the Lord's command, we find the manna the Lord provided in the desert had ceased, and they were eating produce from the land. Joshua was now focused on Jericho, and the Lord again came, and the captain of the Lord's host said to Joshua, "Remove your sandals from your feet, for the place where you are standing is holy."[45]

I believe that it is important to note that the holiness of God is not to be lost in understanding who He is. Apart from His holiness, I don't believe we can truly know Him. He reminds us when called that before anything else, the reverence He expects because of who He is and His holiness should be exhibited: "And Joshua fell on his face to the earth, and bowed down."[46]

What relevance has that for us today, as the Old Covenant has been replaced with a New

Covenant for God's people? Things have certainly changed with the freedom that has been given us in Christ Jesus. But we do know this: our Lord God has not changed, and there has been no diminishing of His holiness. Do we enter the sanctuary of our churches with this reverence? I told one of my closest Christian friends that the next time I am offered the opportunity to preach, I am going to have a rope tied around my waist, and a church leader will hold the end while I walk in front of the congregation. Yes, the veil has been torn from top to bottom, and our access to this holy God is different than when the High Priest, once a year, went into the holy of holies for the people's atonement. But our God is not different, and His holiness remains. I only mention this for the positioning of our hearts and minds as we come to worship our God. He's not really interested in the results of wins and losses in the sports we have watched or played. He's not really interested in who or what needs to be known, except for Him. Yes, our worship will include intercessory prayer but founded in a purpose and person of holiness, and our reverence and motives will be witnessed in heaven.

R. C. Sproul espoused that "holiness is the characteristic of God's nature that is at the very core of His being" and that in this encounter "in His holiness" we will begin to know ourselves as we really are.[47] Isaiah chapter 6 juxtaposes ourselves with a holy God, with angels exhorting one another in repetition of the holiness and glory of God in the fullness of the earth. What are we before a holy God?

Every book of the Bible speaks to the holiness of God. The following verses were selected to help develop our understanding of God's holiness and what it can mean to us and expect of us:

THEMES: THE HOLINESS OF GOD

Below are scripture verses demonstrating the holiness of God exhibited in His kingdom, His words, His name, His character, and His works. Magnified is His holiness in all His creation, in heaven where adoration by His hosts commend earthly saints to imitate. A holiness incomparable to all things revered. A holiness served that becomes the serving, with the whole earth full of His glory, producing a trembling fear of approbation. Found in His promises, holiness is pledged in the power of the Holy Spirit to those who receive and believe in Him, and we praise Him for He has made and judged us holy in our motives, producing an authentic godly fear.

Supporting scripture verses	Theme
Exodus 15:11	Name and sanctifier and exalted above all
Leviticus 19:2; 20:26; 22:32; 44-45	Imparted and infused
1 Samuel 2:2	Incomparable
1 Chronicles 16:35	Savior, deliverer, thanksgiving, glory, and praise
Job 6:10	Undeniable One

Psalm 11:4; 15:1; 22:3; 24:3-4; 33:21	Residence, praise and worship, praiseworthy, person and action, and name
Psalm 60:6; 77:13; 89:35; 93:5; 99:5, 9	Spoken, pledge, service, magnified, praise in song
Proverbs 9:10	Wisdom and understanding
Isaiah 5:16; 6:3; 35:8; 40:25; 43:15; 57:15	Righteousness, The Way, incomparable, sovereignty, omnipotence and humility, glory, and name and adoration
Jeremiah 23:9	His words
Ezekiel 36:23; 38:23	Name: I Am, greatness, and revealing
Joshua 24:19	Service
Habakkuk 2:20	Residence
Amos 4:2	Judgement
Zachariah 2:13	Residence

Luke 1:49; 1:75	Action and His name
John 1:14; 17:11	Glory, relationship, and character
Romans 6:22; 12:1	Benefits and sacrifice
1 Corinthians 3:17	Residence
2 Corinthians 7:1	Fearful perfection
Ephesians 1:4; 2:21; 5:27	Character, body, and residence
Philippians 2:15	Light
Colossians 3:12	Character
1 Thessalonians 4:7	Sanctification
2 Timothy 1:9	Life
Hebrews 2:11; 10:10; 12:14	Sanctification and requirement
1 Peter 1:15-16; 2:9	Resemblance
2 Peter 3:11	Character
1 John 3:3	Hope
Revelation 4:8; 15:4; 22:11	Fearful worship and unceasing praise

The nature of our God has been exposed here, hopefully in such a way that you desire more of Him than when you began reading. Know that He is God, and there is none other—no other God. He is the One and only God. Isaiah's God inspired/spoken words capture the singleness, the oneness, and as one of my closest Christian friends would say, the onliest that makes Him alone as Creator, Sustainer, and Ruler of all creation. He is the painter of life in every form. It is His canvas, and it is lively with the stroke of His brush. "I am the Lord, and there is no other; Besides Me there is no God. I will gird you, though you have not known Me. That men may know from the rising to the setting of the sun that there is no one besides Me. I am the Lord, and there is no other."[48]

God has spoken and identified Himself, and He sent His Son into the world not to condemn the world but to save the world through Him. And as God identifies Himself in word and deed, through His Spirit and life, so does His Son. The religious leaders of His time on earth unknowingly gave us the perfect opportunity to know who He said He was: "'If You are the Christ, tell us.' But He said to them, 'If I tell you, you will not believe; and if I ask a question, you will not answer. But from now on the Son of Man will be seated at the right hand of the power of God.' And they all said, 'So You are the Son of God?' And He said to them, 'You say correctly that I am.'"[49]

You have heard it said before: either Jesus is who He said He is, or He is a liar. Man has, for all time, spoken of who Jesus was and is. Some said that He was John the Baptist, and others have said Elijah or Jeremiah or one of the prophets. Today some simply say Jesus was a person historically—a good person in His time. The Lord, though, responds to such conjecture with a question that not only identifies Him but also the ones who posed the question: "But who do you say that I am?"[50]

It is a question that is ageless. There is no barriered time or statute of limitations. And so the question is asked here: Who do you say that He is? The question searches out nerves that reach the deepest part of our hearts and might generate a reflecting question itself: Well, who do you say that you are?

I like the account of the women He met at a well in a most unlikely place: Samaria. Jesus, being of the lineage of those who would have nothing to do with Samaritans, traveled to the place and made time to do what no Jew would do: meet with and speak to a Samaritan. At that well, His discourse revealed the foundations of our faith: (1) He is the source of living water; (2) He knows us intimately and infinitely more than we know ourselves; (3) God is Spirit, and true worshipers worship Him in spirit and truth; (4) He declares all things; and (5) He declares who He is. "The woman said to Him, 'I know that Messiah is coming (He who is called Christ); when that One comes, He will declare all things to us.' Jesus said to her, 'I am He, the One speaking to you.'"[51] Peter, too, simply acknowledged who Christ is when he answered the question, "'But who do you yourselves say that I am?' Simon Peter answered, 'You are the Christ, the Son of the living God.'"[52]

Our knowledge of God spurs us on in obedience that furthers our knowledge of Him. Thank goodness it is a never-ending cycle that dare not be broken. Our rebellion against our own knowledge of Him is the only thing I know of that can break that cycle, and over time, our hearts will be allowed to harden, and our choices further us from the throne of grace. I am convinced that when that distance becomes great, our Lord will do things to get our attention in ways that we may not desire, for He will not lose one of us who has been made His. When our heart is strong in the confidence of God, there is nothing that can snatch us from His hands. It may take *rock-bottom*, but thank God for such poverty that receives Him back whom He never left. And to receive Him back, oh what joy is this that His name is evermore on our minds and in our hearts—imprinted like a banner. His name is wonderful, Jesus my Lord.[53]

> *Wonderful, Counselor, Mighty God, Eternal Father, Prince of Peace. (Isa. 9:6)*

> *And there is salvation in no one else; for there is no other name under heaven that has been given among men by which we must be saved. (Acts 4:12)*

> *A name high above all other names. For this reason also God highly exalted Him, and bestowed on Him the name which is above every name, so that at the name of Jesus EVERY KNEE WILL BOW, of those who are in heaven and on earth and under the earth, and that every tongue will confess that Jesus Christ is Lord, to the glory of God the Father. (Phil. 2:9-11)*

> *"I am the LORD, that is My name; I will not give My glory to another, Nor My praise to idols." (Isa. 42:8)*

What's in a name? Peter's recorded sermons in the book of Acts site where he, in essence, said that it is our own identity with the Person of Jesus Christ: "Peter said to them, 'Repent, and each of you be baptized in the Name of Jesus Christ for the forgiveness of your sins; and you will receive the gift of the Holy Spirit.'"[54] Peter later records the healing of a lame beggar, crediting it to faith in Jesus and His name: "'And on the basis of faith in His name, it is the name of Jesus which has strengthened this man whom you see and know; and the faith which comes through Him has given him this perfect health in the presence of you all.'"[55]

Names are important, for they can reveal the character of a man. We were given a name at birth, and if we knew or asked, there was meaning behind the choice, reflecting a known or wanted character. Through our journey in life, our walk inspired other names—some nicknames, some spontaneous reflections of the moments of our actions. Some stay with us, and some are lost with our growth and maturing as an adult, no longer reflecting our changed character.

Our name is important to God the Father and our Lord Jesus in the power of the Holy Spirit and to others that we are to know in that relationship. Paul wrote to those in the church of Philippi about friends he knew, fellow workers in the faith: "Indeed, true companion, I ask you also to help these women who have shared my struggle in the cause of the gospel, together with Clement also and the rest of my fellow workers, whose names are in the book of life."[56]

What's in a name? Or should the question be, what's your name in? John, in the book of Revelation, alludes to the true motive of every man in what we worship, and there is a definitive demarcation as to what we worship or whom that is, and names are taken and written down in a book of life—or not. "All who live on the earth will worship him [the dragon, Satan], everyone whose name has not been written since the foundation of the world in the book of life of the Lamb who has been slaughtered."[57]

What's in a name? God's character through the ages has been revealed in His given names:

Yahweh-Sabbaoth	The Lord of Hosts; Captain of the armies of heaven
Yahweeh-Ghmolah	The God of recompense: "vengeance is mine"
Elohim	God is Creator
El-Elyon	The Most High God
El-Gibhor	Mighty God

El-Olam	The Everlasting God
El-Roi	The Strong One Who Sees
El-Shaddai-Rohi	God Almighty; the Mighty One of Jacob
El-Chuwl	The God Who Gave Birth; God is our Creator and our Father
El-Deah	God of Knowledge; Wisdom Comes from the Lord
Attiyq Youm	The Ancient of Days; God is Eternal
El Shaddai	All-Sufficient One
I Am	The Very Name of God
Yahweh	Self-Existent One
Adonai	Lord Over All; He Is King of kings and Lord of lords; He Reigns Forever

Yahweh-Maccaddeshem	The Lord Your Sanctifier; He Forgives Your Sins
Yahweh-Rohi	The Lord My Shepherd; He Cares for You
Yahweh-Shammah	The Lord Who Is Present; He Never Leaves You Nor Forsakes You; He is with You Forever
Yahweh-Rapha	The Lord Our Healer
Yahweh-Tsidkenu	The Lord Our Righteousness
Yahweh-Jireh	The Lord Will Provide
Yahweh-Nissi	The Lord Our Banner
Yahweh-Shalom	The Lord Is Peace

*Note that some, in reference, substitute the name *Jehovah* for *Yahweh* in humble preference.

Digesting the names of God that have been given by His chosen help us to grasp onto that which we can exceedingly know—the character of our God, God Himself revealed in a Person of whom He is. The names reflect not only who He is but what He has done as well. We become fully orbed, knowing Him, and as I close this last chapter (of Part 1), let me say: *Shalom.*

It has been my most high privilege and pleasure to share with you these pages and my prayer is that you continue to seek to know our Lord more and more every day, building a deeper and deeper relationship, being blessed to the core of your being. Let the sun not go down without venturing further into the heart of our God. May it be said of us, "They were one with a heart after God."

Shalom.

PART 2:
DISLOCATED HIP

Genesis 32:24-32

MY BODY

This title should certainly conjure up a lot of brain activity. We hear those two words more today than I think we ever have in all of history. So many different directions are opened up in the channels of thinking, yet one overriding theme usually takes place front and center. It can be an obvious observation or subtle as a service engine light on your dash. But either way, there could be an underlying motive stemming from a prideful heart. Think of these two interactions with the mind and the heart:

1. Admiration with oneself

2. Authority of oneself

Or it could be a crying from the soul, where these interactions may best identify the internal transaction:

1. Pleading with oneself

2. Pleading with others

3. Despair from who knows where

4. Sickness, hurting, asking why

There are many more, I'm sure, but there is a juxtaposition of the ageless pride and humility in character that can expose motives within oneself.

We claim who we are, and they claim who they are, and we each exclaim who the other is in many dimensions. It can be related to friendships, it can be political association, sports teams, clubs, or any competitive arena. It can be communities or countries that we are quick to compare and often without any real knowledge to assert real differences. And often it is to promote that the other is not equal to us, and we are better than they are.

It can even be religion and the church. That reflection is one with crucial overtones that can lead to discord, divisions, and schisms within "my body," Jesus would say. There it is. . . .

We claim who we are, and we claim who they are, when we should claim who He is. And if I may, this might be a good place to interject our Lord's perspective regarding our body, considering He made it. No matter our walk in life; our circumstances; or the environment of economic, social, or community that influences our perspective, it is always good and always best to consider others and their perspective(s). So here is our Lord's written perspective, a godly perspective of our body:

> *"Or do you not know that your body is the temple of the Holy Spirit who is in you, whom you received from God? You are not your own, you were bought at a price [a very high price,*

> *I might add], therefore glorify God with your body."* (1 Cor. 6:19)

So, does that influence our own perspective of "my body"? Is there agreement? I'm pretty sure that any disagreement would lead to an authority conflict. Can we not be our own? Watch any protest for the legalization of abortions, and you will not miss the "my body" shouts, signs, and assured proclamations.

14

THE TRUTH

Really? Most of us recognize there is nothing greater than our God, as He demonstrated for Elijah before the prophets of Baal. This, too, does not go unnoticed, that revealing Himself as the One and True God is needed before men, and there will be the rest of the story as He desires in His time and place, even choosing just one of us to deliver and demonstrate [THE TRUTH].

I will let that linger in your minds at this point and move on because that is just the horizon of the implications of "my body," which has far greater meaning, reaching beyond the physical and bringing together the wholeness of our actual life where the spirit is often willing, but the flesh is weak.

When Christ says, "My body" (not anything like your body, in reference), He is referring to His body, the church. He reveals much, speaking allegorically so that we grasp the essence of the unity He so desires, recognizing that there are many differences but working in concert so that the body functions as one.

I have a unique perspective in the life of Christ's body, and it has been one that continues to evolve with the passing of the years. I was born into a Presbyterian family, and my early childhood would be molded around traditional Presbyterian doctrine, those years bringing out some of the most enjoyable times that are embedded in memory. I was three years old when my mom would drop me off Saturday mornings in the basement of Third Presbyterian

Church in Ft. Wayne, Indiana. We would watch a Christian movie, and there would be candy bars that would help entice coming back each week. We would sing the childhood songs many of you may have also sung at an early age, at least those of you who are nudging your twilight years. I remember the very first song we were taught (amazing how those things stay with us): "Jesus Walked This Lonesome Valley."

It would not be long before our parents would move us four children to Ft. Lauderdale, Florida (thank you, Mom and Dad), in 1955, and I remember the trip vividly. My mom drove us alone in a Packard panel/delivery truck. I only remember the one stop we made on the Florida Turnpike when my mom bought breakfast for us but not for herself—an early lesson she didn't even know she was teaching me.

For more than twenty years, and through my first two years of college, Ft. Lauderdale would be my home. During my first year, I met a sweetheart that would impact the rest of my life's faith journey, unbeknownst to her. I was a Presbyterian; she and her family were not. You probably know how affection can guide your mind in accepting differences, and these, for me, would be a significant challenge based on learned prejudices that I accepted, considering what I thought were shared truths. Mercy me, she and her family were Catholic; my faith—your faith—are they the same? I am convinced by all biblical accounts that they are, but could our differences in traditions and rituals lead to a bodily (body of Christ) dysfunction?

> *He said to them: "You are well aware that it is against our law for a Jew to associate with or visit a Gentile. But God has shown me that I should not call anyone impure or unclean." (Acts 10:28)*

> *Opening his mouth, Peter said: "I most certainly understand now that God is not one to show partiality, but in every nation the man who fears Him and does what is right is acceptable to Him." (Acts 10:34-35)*

The walls we have created from our traditions in worship and ritual that summarily divide us, God has broken down so that we can fellowship together as He so desires—as one in Him, His body, the church. "His divine power has given us everything we need for life and godliness through our knowledge of Him who has called us by His own glory and goodness."[58] Everything we need is given to us to bridge the differences and edify the church, building everyone up in the body of Christ to the praise and glory of His name and the good of all of His church.

15

TRADITIONAL SPICES

The sweetheart relationship would continue until my second year of college in 1971, when I was drafted into the Army. It was the first year that they did away with college deferments and went to a lottery selection of who would be mandated into service. I remember it well, as my number was the very last number to be drawn in the lottery—not a win I was fond of at the time.

During that relationship, short as it was, I would be challenged with my faith conceptions—an application of faith, if you will. How do we apply what we know about our faith, what we know in faith? Who are we, and what do we look like? How do we express ourselves in faith? The answers to these most intimate questions ultimately lead to edifying the body of Christ or a breakdown in holy principles we assure ourselves that we know.

I remember early on in the relationship I was invited to join them in church, and looking back on that first time I went with them, I am humbled that they would ask me more than once. A liturgical mass: what was that? I had never experienced that before. Readings from the Old and New Testament I understood, but the connection of singing additional scripture and the kneeling (and quite often), it just seemed rudimentary, and surely (I thought) you don't have to get on your knees to pray. Surely the Lord would hear my prayer sitting as well as kneeling. Maybe, maybe not, looking back. For the condition of the heart is the litmus test. *Forgive me, Lord,* is my reflection now, as I am sure a subtle pride found its way into my rationalization. The psalmist wrote, "The sacrifices of God is a broken spirit. A broken and contrite heart he will not despise."[59] There was no brokenness on my part, only my way of tradition in the Presbyterian nurturing. I remember our pastor's son once telling me while we were standing and praying that he prayed with his eyes open.

To not get too many stones thrown at me at this point, prayer can find its way in just about any form. But if our eyes are wide open, I am confident that we are far more susceptible to distractions that can injure the brokenness of the heart that gets our Lord's attention. Jesus Himself said, "When you pray, go into your room and shut the door and pray to your Father in Heaven who is in secret."[60] Why? Many times, Jesus would go remotely to pray to the Father. Why? We know the answer. Prayer is a most intimate time when we can be with our Lord. We are speaking to Creator God, King of kings, Lord of lords, Sustainer of all life in every form. We may be casual, but if we are, may it be because we are so close to God that we call Him *Master,* and we are with Him always, inseparable. Where He is, we are, and our faith is simply a way of life, a living sacrifice pleasing to Him. Paul urged that to all believers, to all followers of Christ, in his letter to the church in Rome.[61] He called them "brothers." That would identify a family, though I'm confident they had different mothers and fathers. A relationship of belonging to one another. They would have the same faith genes, forming a unified and common body in faith.

There's the opening to the spices we add to the holy church of God. Spices that should enhance our faith to taste delicious and build it strong. There is a warning label on the spices, though. Using the wrong way can lead to ruining the very food set before us, and we never eat the same way together because our taste is what now dictates if we will even eat the food.

Let's list some of the denominational spices that have conditioned our taste buds to influence our hearts and minds:

- The Sabbath Day
- Sacraments, ordinances, God-ordained ceremonies
- Baptism
- Communion celebration, the Lord's Supper, the Eucharist, the Bread and the Wine
- Confession of sins
- Indulgences, penance
- Marriage and divorce
- Church membership, confirmation
- Church order, liturgy
- Church leadership and authority
- Deacons and elders
- Anointings
- Commitment and service
- Faith and works
- Statues and images
- Mary and veneration
- Sons of Joseph and Mary, brothers of Jesus

- Heaven, purgatory
- Books of the Bible (Apocrypha)
- Signing of the cross
- Prayer and methods

I only list these to detail that all of the differences that exist in the church today would be limitless and would certainly result in use to further delineate the sides that are taken to justify our notions of what is right and what is wrong. I do suggest that if we debate any or all of the above that we debate from the side we least agree with. That is, that we research the topic from the other side—the scriptural basis for the doctrine and posits—to be sure we have an accurate understanding and not just a possible conjecture that is misguided. This is not to change any minds but to have a thorough understanding that allows bridges to be built over the chasms that leave us divided and dysfunctional in walking together as our Lord so desires. John writes the words of Jesus regarding this desire: "The glory which You have given Me I have given to them, that they may be one, just as We are one; I in them and You in Me, that they may be perfected in unity so that the world may know that You sent Me, and loved them, even as You have loved Me."[62] That is our aim (or it should be), our goal, that we may be one just as the Father and Son—perfected in unity. Why? So that the world may know that Jesus was sent for an eternal purpose: the salvation of our souls.

How is that perfect unity achieved with so many differences? How do the divisions that we perpetuate edify the body, building each other up?

I can only use my experience to qualify any comment or encouragement. I used to exclaim that the Lord has a unique sense of humor, but it is much deeper than a humorous comment. It is His focus on a particular need by one whom He loves and desires to know Him and His way. My exclamation by explanation was that His dealing with me would be, *Keep acting this way with your prejudices and misgivings, and I will see to it that you marry a Catholic.* And after forty-five years of marriage, I am most grateful that He did just that.

16

BORN TOGETHER

The previous chapter disclosed what would be faith-challenging times in a new crossbreeding of faith in marriage. I say *new*, but Solomon is right, there is nothing new under the sun, as we find reading through the Old Testament. That said, bringing us to more current times, my wife was and is a committed evangelical Catholic, and I was and am a committed evangelical Protestant/Catholic or Catholic/Protestant, whichever stirs the partiality in one's blood. The question is, how in the world was that going to work?

During our engagement, we were required to take a course (that is, if I was going to marry the one I fell in love with—a guided love, I am convinced) of consultation called Pre-Cana. The name is derived from John 2:1-12, the wedding feast at Cana in Galilee, where Jesus performed the miracle of turning water into wine. We, together, decided that if we were to marry, we would not impose our faith traditions upon the other or try to change the spices of traditions that provided for growth and maturity in the faith— "A Closer Walk with Thee," you may sing. That would prove to be a great foundational axiom that would lead to, in our lives, growing closer and closer to our Lord in understanding, faith, hope, and love. I studied in detail every concept, every precept, every principle, every scriptural basis for doctrine in the Catholic catechism to be able to ask questions and to be able to understand what was about to happen regarding the ordination of a blessed marriage. I remember during the marriage course and meetings with the parish priest, his surprise that anyone would do that, and I surmised that most of those in the course simply ritualistically saw this as a process for qualifying to marry with the blessings of the church.

That would be the beginning of understanding that would attack my preconceived notions about Catholics and the Catholic church. I could not begin to tell you all of the steps in learning I (and my wife) have made during the past forty-five years and counting. What I can say is that the basics of our faith in Christ, the Son of God, Messiah, Deliverer, Savior, Redeemer, risen Lord, is without difference: one faith, one true God.

Our Lord's heart is for unity in His body. There is no argument regarding that charge to the church. The question is how we bring about that unity with all of the differences we see in our divisive world. Division is not of God's planning, at least in His body. But He does have an enemy, an adversary that is pretty good at dividing and conquering. Throughout scripture, God has revealed His design for relationships and connecting dots that seem far apart. We can engage in relationships where we can experience more of who God is and all He has for us, edifying His body, building each other up, or we can use differences to tear each other down in accusations that become stumbling blocks to growing in knowledge of our Lord to be more and more like Him.

Our marriage has been one of many bridges, and I can attest that I would be nowhere near the maturity in faith that I am if I had been secluded from all that I have experienced in a marriage that has brought unity where two have truly become one.

It began with a love that yielded a yearning for understanding. A desire to bring together and build the strongest marriage possible under the tutelage and guidance of our Lord and His Word in ways that were not traditional.

We were blessed with three children, and because of our vow to each other in this faith exercise, we would attend two churches and not just on Sundays. We would involve ourselves in the churches as if each was our only church. Our children were baptized in the Catholic church with our Presbyterian pastor as part of the proceedings. I would become a Sunday school teacher and deacon in the Presbyterian church, and my wife (Barbara, hereinafter) would teach at VBS at both churches. I remember my children telling me later in years as teenagers that growing up, they thought that all families and their children went to two churches. You may ask how we did that, and looking back, the only explanation is by the grace of God and His planning and provision because it always worked out flawlessly wherever we lived. And we moved often, living in Slidell, LA; Harmony, PA; Peachtree City, GA; Weddington and Garner, NC; and Collierville, TN.

While in Garner, there came a time where the Catholic church and Barbara wanted me to become an attending member. I was a member at that time of Aversboro Baptist Church. I told the parish course advisor and priest that I would be happy to go through the catechumen process of comprehensive catechesis on the truths of Catholic doctrine and moral life, and as with the Pre-Cana marriage course, I would study in detail all aspects of the teachings. I remember initially, I was the only one that would bring my Bible to the meetings and share scripture with other catechumens that supported the doctrine postulates. Somewhere during the course, others started bringing their Bibles as well. When the course was finished, I was asked if I was going to join the church, and I said I would be happy to but would not rescind my membership at the Baptist church. It took special dispensation, but the bishop of the Diocese approved the membership, and I became a member of St. Mary's Catholic Church in Garner, NC. I was a member of the choir at Aversboro and also became a member of the choir at St. Mary's. That was always one of the bridges in our marriage—singing with both choirs. Teaching and ministering in prayer and missions in both churches was also an interchurch highway that would lead to promised peace and security. Thirty-two years of prison ministry would also open doors to ministry of understanding that would encourage a broadened populace, seeking our Lord in truths that would break chains of slavery to be truly freed from bondage.

When we are born again (1 Pet. 1:3: "Blessed be the Father of our Lord Jesus Christ who has caused us to be born again to a living hope through the resurrection of Jesus Christ from the dead"), we are born together in one body, Jesus Christ—us in Him and Him in us—and we become family (John 1:12: "To those who receive Him, to those who believe in His name, He gives the right to become children of God. Children born not of natural descent, nor of human decision, or a husband's will, but born of God"). A perfect unity is made in Him because we are born together in one body. Jesus said, "Whoever does the will of my Father in Heaven, he is my brother, he is my sister, he is my mother" (Mark 3:35). I believe that is one of the reasons Jesus, from the cross, said to His earthly mother, Mary, "Behold your son," and He said to John, "Behold your mother" (John 19:27). From that moment on, John took Mary into his household. It isn't that Jesus as some earthly legal judge made a legal determination that would legitimize an otherwise unconsidered relationship; it was a recognition of the family relationship we have as believers in Him and the responsibilities that are carried with that.

Together in Him, born again in the likeness of Christ Jesus, is the identification that can't be missed when others see the same in you and me.

17

SURGICAL SEPARATION

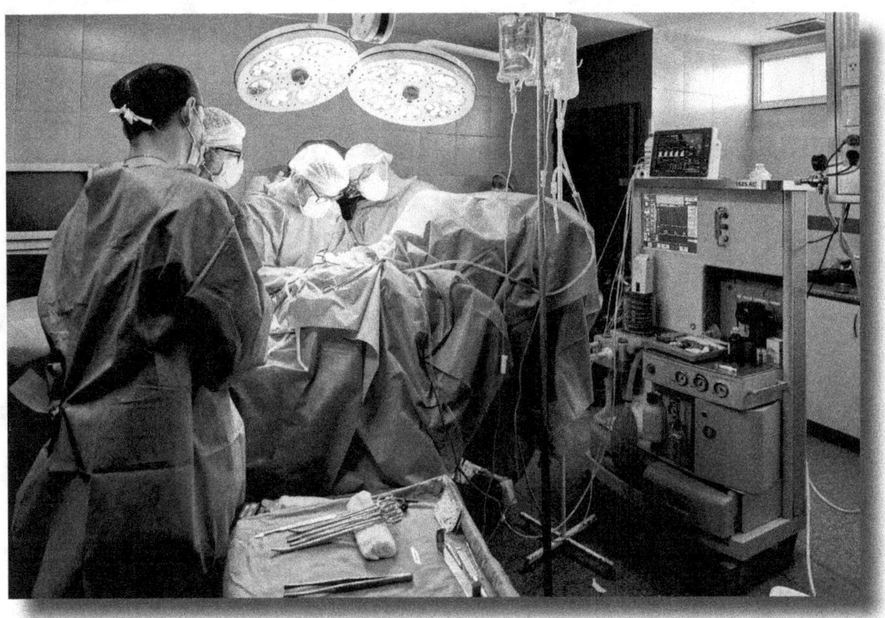

Jesus' ascension to heaven was the beginning of a new day. It was a new birth of not one but many, and the church would find its roots in His disciples and the many who believed in sharing His gospel truths that are the bedrock of our faith today. Even in the earliest stages of church growth, there would be challenges to the unity Jesus prayed for and so desired of His people. From the time of Creation itself, the evil adversary would constantly influence and deceive those who would attack the unity of believers, and the age-old adage of "divide and conquer" would reflect what I believe is the devil's foundational strategy that wreaks havoc in the fellowship of believers. Little differences would build into mountains of heresy, and doctrine would be canonized to hold truths. Traditions would be established to help keep doctrinal focus, but not without warning. Beware, traditions cannot add to scripture truths; they can only be based on scripture truths. They are not scripture truths in and of themselves. We do not worship our traditions. We worship the One and Only True God who alone is worthy of our worship. It is a warning to the church in Christ and for all time. Differences in tradition can be a harvest field for the evil one to deceive and divide, to divide and to conquer, to conquer and destroy. We do have many protective promises that when the rubber meets the road, "He who is in us is greater than he who is in the world."[63]

One could argue there have always been challenges to the church and its doctrine. Early organized sects would declare their beliefs alone held the truths and the secret key to religious order, despising all others. Referred to some as Gnostic beliefs, Paul would encounter and oppose their teachings in his letters to churches in Colossae and Corinth. From the late first century to the middle of the second, orthodox leaders would contend with Gnostics, trying to convert true believers to a secrecy in religion that was their own. They rejected the incarnation of Christ and the belief of His being wholly man and wholly God, a heresy known as Docetism. Radical biblical criticism would generate canons from rationalizations that would distort what Jesus taught. Salvation would only be offered to an elite few.

Paul, a faithful teacher of truths, wrote in his letter to Timothy that petitions, prayers, intercession, and thanksgiving should be made for all people:

> *This is good and pleases God our Savior, who wants all people to be saved and to come to a knowledge of the truth. For there is one God and one mediator between God and mankind, the man*

> *Christ Jesus, who gave himself as a ransom for all people. This has now been witnessed to at the proper time. And for this purpose, I was appointed a herald and an apostle—I am telling the truth, I am not lying—and a true and faithful teacher to the Gentiles. (1 Tim. 2:1-7)*

Spiritual surgery would be required from the earliest of times to remove heresy from the church to remain pure and holy, sanctified in the truths taught by our Lord Jesus. The sects throughout history would come but would not remain, for their own lies would find them out and leave them estranged from the true church. This sanctification and standing firm in truthful doctrine in faith would also create much dissention and from earliest times would lead to well-known Christian persecution.

We could fast-forward to a discussion of the reformation that would bypass many of the continuous challenges within and outside of the church. That period would be a catalyst to many of our Protestant church denominations of today. But these pages are not a study in systematic theology; they are simply written to bring additional light to the challenges we face in keeping the unity our Lord Jesus Christ says is His body.

It took a surgical effort to separate Christians from the foundational truths that unify the body, and it has been an operational effort that I believe the evil one continues today and will for all time until our Lord returns. At that time, all power to the surgery room will be cut off, and the surgeon will be cast out, and true unity will return. But in the meantime, we, by the power of the Holy Spirit, can overcome our differences, focus on the scriptural truths, and build bridges of faith. I am confident in this because if He can do it in one marriage, He can and will do it in the marriage of the Lamb.

18

FINDING A WAY

We live with many preferences that we feel lead to a way of peace and stability, weeding out our uncertainties that can cloud the day with unanticipated needs and worries. Some preferences are simple in demonstration, like where you sit in class if you are a student or where you might sit in church on Sundays. There are repeated patterns of behavior because of the influential preferences that may be subtle and unrecognized unless addressed or questioned.

Some we plan; some come, we feel, naturally; and some handed from generation to generation surprise us in our identity until we reflect the possible preferential origin. We've all heard the colloquialism, "The apple doesn't fall far from the tree." That suggests that we are rooted in a preferential behavior that finds its origin in one before us with influential values that have been accepted and now expressed in similar behavior.

The majority of church denominational preferences have been passed on from generation to generation with children accepting the faith practices of their parents. It is a cohesive family unit undisturbed during adolescent years because of parent-child relationships that provide for the needs of children and parents alike. The necessary unity—thinking alike, acting alike, a well-synchronized orchestration of daily life—leads to a peaceful existence that provides for growth and maturity that is not encumbered with battles of disagreement.

That is the early years, but in every case, there comes a time in the family where challenges arise to understanding and authority regarding behaviors that test the boundaries of *the way*. Other influences find their way into the family-established way of life, and even core values can be challenged. Finding a way of their own can be expected as children mature, and they find themselves in a position of influence. These are the most critical years of transition and can result in a life that is arbitrarily influenced or a life that influences and in the science of things resembles introvert or extrovert behavior.

It is interesting that many organizations take on this family behavioral dichotomy, and we find church denominations vastly different in their worship practices. We can identify challenges that are dysfunctional to the body and lead to separations that are hurtful but thankfully survivable. Finding a way where bridges have been built to span disruptive currents and walking to the other side finds a road in likeness that leads further down the path we so desire to travel.

Think about those bridges in construction and in life. They are reinforced for maximum strength far beyond the needed strength to provide safety and security. The foundation is deep and can withstand torrents of unexpected weather. They can span the greatest of chasms with seemingly no limit to one's vision of continuing down the road. They are not built by any one individual; they are built by those committed to making the vision a reality, a team of many with a common goal, working together. Though many differences in skills, they have learned to work together and produce what no one could do on their own.

Where are the bridge builders in the church today? Can anyone orchestrate the many different instruments to produce a symphony of chorus that will leave everyone individually wanting to be a part of the production? We know what the sound can be. We know what the sound should be and the resulting music that resonates to the heavens.

The foundation exists to make good music. Finding a way to build that bridge of strength with all the different skills working together is not a dead-end dream. Finishing such needed construction will find an orchestra playing and tape being cut in celebration for the opening of travelers continuing on the road to unity.

We have to find a way. It's the only way. Unity in the body of Christ, the church, must be a priority with a focused effort that says, *Not my way but the Lord's way.* Us in Him and He in us with the signature of the Lord on every heart. With an identity that edifies the church and leads others to cross the bridge and travel the road leading to the knowledge of the Lord our God. Finding a way is the only way.

19

WHO'S DIFFERENT?

Some may feel it comes naturally to notice things that are different rather than the same, and though there may be a plethora of good things that have been done, one error stands out as if it were the only thing that transpired in a forest of actions and words in summary of our attention.

It may be our own status that regulates the analytical process of judgmental prowess. After all, being held in high esteem most often comes at the price of one's own sacrifice or another's. Character traits are not always easily recognizable in anxious moments, and fleeting may be ones that demonstrate a denial of self and a humble sacrificing when the good of another is the goal. Those times and responses generated from motives that dictate our behavior come frequently before us, constantly testing who we are. Our Lord is not silent regarding our identifying character, and His Word cannot be distorted by rationalizing the circumstances. Paul exhorted His words to the congregation in Philippi: "Do nothing out of selfish ambition or vain conceit, but in humility consider others better than yourselves."[64] Arguing the natural tendency is to elevate our position, which may include the lowering of another, resonates with the achiever at all costs—the winner, champion of champions.

Knowing who we are does not come with self-analysis alone. We actually have to know others before we can fully know ourselves, and the ultimate full knowledge of oneself never comes without knowing Christ our Lord. Truly knowing Him reveals ourselves in a way that the world and we can never know apart from Him. Knowing Him reveals characteristics in us that guide our decisions, being intentionally decisive through devotion and discipline with a determination and diligence that molds the likeness in image of our Lord Jesus Christ. Having the mind of Christ is more than a repeated challenge; it becomes a way of life in faith that is just the way we are without thinking, and we know others in the same light. The remarkable thing is that this transcends man-constructed barriers that define us as different—Catholic, Baptist, Lutheran, Methodist, Episcopalian, to include hundreds more. The help for that supernatural transcendence is the Holy Spirit, the commonality that never changes, and the hope for the unity that can be—yes unity that can be.

Who's different? We all are, yet we are the same in Christ. Think about it. It was and is prayed for today, and the will of our Lord will not be denied. What is it that we are waiting for? For others to be exactly like us and think exactly as we do? It will never happen. So what can bring about the will of God, the unity in the body? Well, I believe that every true Christian would agree that understanding is simply found in obedience—the difficulty being one of execution. Denying oneself and taking up our cross and following Him as the Master of all things in us does prove challenging at times. Letting go and letting God takes on a meaning of more than just words to satisfy a grieving soul. We can take time out to identify the common place amongst differences we so want to use to justify a dividing attitude. What does that time-out look like in faith applied in practical ways? The list may be longer than you think and is not limited to the suggestions below:

- Prayer

- Scripture

- Fellowship

- Circumstances

Practical experience can be found historically in revivals and crusades where thousands, even hundreds of thousands, have gathered in the name of Christ. That fellowship has virtually nearly every known faith denomination created in the church, and worship and praise become commonplace. The power of the Holy Spirit is vibrant, threading lives together that would never otherwise meet. Who's different? No one, for all have fallen short of the glory of God. But God has demonstrated His love for us, and the cross becomes the bridge that finds our likeness in the holiness of God. "But now, God has reconciled us by Christ's physical body through death, to present us holy in His sight, without blemish and free from accusation." Are we not the same because of Him? Who's different?[65]

20

FRIENDLY FIRE

Christians and the fellowship, the church, expects hateful challenges from worldly aisles of contention, for the handwriting is on the wall, or should we say, in the scrolls. It is written that there will be persecution that will be ramped up in later days. Jesus said, "You will be hated by everyone because of Me, but the one who stands firm to the end will be saved. When you are persecuted in one place, flee to another."[66] Reflecting on the known persecution of our Master in Jesus Christ, His exhorted truth ("The disciple is not above his master, nor the servant above his lord"[67]), leads to an expectancy of intolerance that carries from generation to generation, and escaping such is not a realistic view of things to come.

But . . . the expected should not be the real concern within the body of Christ, the church. Concerning is the biting and gnashing that has found its way into the sanctuary, where unity is slashed with an unleashed fervor that dismembers parts, leaving an inability to witness to the unity needed to function and grow.

The entire law of the profits is fulfilled by keeping one command of our Lord: "Love your neighbor as yourself."[68] And we are told that "if you bite and devour each other, watch out or you will be destroyed by each other."[69]

We know one called the *destroyer,* and division within the body of Christ is a goal of destruction as ancient as the serpent himself. "Watch out" is not a subtle inference but a screaming warning as if peril is at the doorstep. Most differences that lead to division are lined with misunderstandings. Hearsay resonates in ears that are ready to hear what fertilizes the misconceptions in confirmation and new rhetoric that fuels a bias justified without true knowledge. Soon fear enters, reasoning to protect and preserve divisive notions. Objectivity becomes lost in a forest of unquestioning dogma, and lost is the notion that Jesus calls us *friends*. To whom does He call friends? Those who know Him. "I no longer call you servants, because a servant does not know his master's business. Instead, I have called you friends, for everything that I learned from my Father I have made known to you."[70]

Reading this, you may feel this is reaching to find a problem that just does not exist and that believers readily and objectively accept other believers and their differences. But I can tell you from forty-five years of experience in a Catholic-Protestant-Baptist household that is full-time-membership serving in these denominations that the confrontations and divisive nature is sadly real—both sides being guilty of unfounded attacks against largely misunderstood traditions and faith differences made to be stumbling blocks rather than building each other up in the brotherhood.

I believe the first step to a needed healing that edifies the body is to eliminate the friendly fire. Our lives together in unity become the good news of the gospel in fulfillment through neighborly love. This is the God I know will thread through all corners of the church, and Jesus answers, *yes, I am the Son of God.*[71]

The only friendly fire that should be is the charcoal fire on the beach that morning when Jesus said, "Come and have breakfast."[72] And this is an invitation that persists today to all who recognize Him and desire to be fed an everlasting meal. Then, when finished eating, a question probes the deep, deep love that loves without bounds: "Do you love Me?"[73]

21

FOR CRYING OUT LOUD

We have all been there with nowhere to go, with no one to hear, with no one to understand, and we cry. The tears flow with despair at the door. There are no words, only the cry, and loudly we beg for help not knowing what help we even need. Who could understand any way to provide what we do not know we need? But for crying out loud, there are ears that hear, and there are eyes upon the suffering, and we come face to face with that which we cannot see.

If My people, the Lord says. "If My people, who are called by my name, will humble themselves and pray and seek My face, and turn from their wicked ways, then will I hear from heaven and forgive their sins and heal their land."[74] We can hear the plea and then know the conviction followed by the cry of all in recognition of the condition, realizing that it starts with me. And oh, how can it be contained, the cry of the poor? Jesus said, "Blessed are the poor for theirs is the Kingdom of Heaven. Blessed are the humble, the kind, the meek for they shall inherit the earth."[75]

What is it that we seek in our cry? Is it relief from pain, sorrow, or persecution? Is there injustice that will not cease, and the heavy burden has brought us to our knees?

Our God is a compassionate God, and we know that our sorrow and pain grieves Him.

Our God is a just God, and we know that injustices do not please Him. He has said, "Now, will not God bring about justice for His elect who cry out to Him day and night, and will He delay long over them?"[76]

The Lord has shown a legacy of regard for our cry, though sometimes it can be an errant cry of jealousy that rewards us with less than His pleasure. We witnessed that in the account of His people, Israel, wanting an earthly king like other nations: "For I have regarded My people, because their cry has come to me."[77]

For what, for where, for when, and for why do we cry, cry out to the Lord? Most likely those questions go unanswered in such a moment. Exasperation may have consumed us. Fear may have gripped us. Sadness may have drowned us in our own tears. Grief may have overwhelmed our senses. But all of what is echoing in the cry does not defeat us because of the hope that does not leave our souls. It is that hope that ignites the cry. It is that hope that keeps us from despair. It is that hope residing in a light that dispels the darkest of dark, and a shadow of another appears in our hearts. The faithful cry of the prayerful elicits a patient, persevering, divinely appointed ability to overcome, and we know our cry has the regard of our God.

For crying out loud, our Lord hears, and His divine power gives us everything we need. Our lives are godlike in response through our knowledge of Him who has called us by His own glory and goodness. For crying out loud, what on earth are we doing for His sake? The inflicted pain is diminished with a purpose found in serving Him.

Yes, our cry should be shrouded in a blanket of service that will bring honor and glory to His name. A cry for help can lift us up, not leaving us incapacitated but effective and productive in a harrowing storm, and we stand, and we conquer, and the storm always passes. A cry for justice can know that it has already been served and awaits the persevering sufferer with a crown of righteousness. Simply crying out loud invites the one we know to hold and to cherish a treasured possession as He promised, and peace begins to flow through us like none known before.

For crying out loud, *come to Me,* says the Lord. *I will wipe away every tear. Fear death no more. Mourning, crying, and pain will have passed away with the old order of things, and a new day of rejoicing is in the morning. Rejoice! Again, for crying out loud, I say rejoice.*

22

THE HURT

What is it that is most hurtful? Is it physical pain where the body's injury is insurmountable? There are medicines that can diminish, even eliminate all physical pain, interrupting a most grievous condition. Is it mental anguish that brings on despair that emotionally can ruin the mind even to death?

Most often remedies treat the symptoms because the cause is elusive to any understanding of any cure and most likely one that does not exist. So the hurt may be masked, but underlying causes remain.

There is no sense in seeking happiness, for any relief is temporary. Hope is fleeting if it is in temporal solutions that can leave us wanting to give up with the repeated hallow remedies.

When pain remains, a change in season is at hand. Life will continue, but it is not the same, and there are only two roads that can be traveled into the forest of no return. One road seems right because there just doesn't seem to be any alternative. We are tempted to wallow in the muddy trenches as the road deteriorates the farther we travel to where the end comes quickly. But there is another road, a road less traveled with seemingly barren stretches that are as far as the eye can see. It is a road that requires courage we feel we do not have, and the fight will be on from the first step taken. A warrior mentality must be adorned with armor in full battle array because we are traveling with a newly partnered pain that somehow, we know will be transformed—not eliminated, but transformed into a new way of thinking, a new way of experiencing, used to motivate life-giving blood to flow like never before.

It doesn't matter whether the hurt is physical or psychological, for the choice remains the same in overcoming. It is the eternal mind that ushers in, choosing a road that leads to a rewarding crown of life accompanied with the thorns gathered along the way. Perfect healing does await when finished traveling, and looking far ahead always excites the harder run with strength we know not of. The encouragement grows, and we know we can do this once we are on the right road. What once was holding us down now builds us up, and a thankfulness once silent cannot be held any longer. We become weary of holding it in, and we ourselves become the encouragement—we become a channel of our Lord's desired healing for another who is hurting just like us. We have been in their shoes and have hurt as they are hurting. It is an identity that can bring the healing power of Christ through words of encouragement to overcome as we have overcome. We can bring the soothing peace of Christ that enables the endurance needed to journey through difficult times.

Can we think of a lingering hurt that has changed our lives forever? There are men (and women) who, with every part of them, witnessed to the love of Christ. I know a married man with, of course, a wife, who gave birth to blessed children. He would train them up in the way they should go, knowing the promise that they would not depart from it later in life. He would teach, he would admonish, he would lead, he would provide, he would protect, and he would give lavishly; yet as the children would depart and travel their own roads, one would depart from a way most desired by the father. A son would choose ways that grieved the father, yet his father's love would only grow. Unceasing prayer would accompany the hurt the father experienced, and the father would question what and where failure might have led the son away. Choices made would be life-changing, and now the future would be different than the father's wanton expectations. The father would search God's words for understanding, and comfort for understanding on his own would not come. What were the reasons? The most deepening hurt was found in the rejection of "the way"— the way of his father's teaching and example and knowing that now some things might not be reversed.

Where was the ointment for the sore of the soul? There are few solutions for physical changes that would transpire, but physical changes do not last an eternity. The father continues to witness to the soul, and his hope is in the spiritual conquest that is always at the door to be opened for a meal where an endless love awaits. And oh, what joy that would bring. Life has changed on earth, but only for a short while. Joyful in hope, with patience brought about in love, and faithfulness in prayer has put the hurt where it belongs. It's not absent but used to strengthen one's battle in pursuit of drawing one home to celebrate a return that will be forever.

The hurt is always a blessing, but it is so deeply rooted in understanding that some never obtain the blessing because the search is so shallow. The appropriate question is not *why* unless we are asking the Lord to reveal Himself to us so that we can understand His perfect will in what He is teaching us for our good. He says, come to Me all ye who are weary and burdened. It is an invitation of promise, a promise of rest from the torment, from the hurt. He says take my yoke and learn from Me. We try to learn from so many places, and today we search the internet as if it was our god. Our Lord waits because so many times He is the last place of resort after we have exhausted our own efforts. He says He is gentle and humble in heart. It was the ultimate humility that hung on the cross. A gentle giant, demonstrating to the world an unmatched sacrifice of love who could understand the pain, the hurt of rejection that would lead to eternal paradise. He said His yoke is easy and His burden is light. So what should we desire? Our yoke and burden of pain, suffering, and hurt, or His yoke and burden, which He has offered to this father and everyone else who is hurting? His leads to rejoicing, though hurt remains. How can that be? Ask the father in the account above, or simply ask the Father above.

PATIENT IN AFFLICTION

No way! This is not human. How can such a request be made or stated? Well, we have to search the original meaning and context of just what that means. It does carry the undertone of perseverance, but how is that achieved? It is a holding fast without retreat, losing ground, and it comes surrounded by practical notions that are the glue of the soul. Joyful in hope, rejoicing in the hope of knowing that this too shall pass, with new tendons constructed from the pressure released against us. We emerge stronger like a butterfly from its struggle in the cocoon. Without the struggle, the colors would never be as bright and beautiful. Without the struggle, there would be no flight.

We are amazed by such simple beauty but seldom reflect on what it took to create such. It is hard to imagine the struggle or even think about it when witnessing such beauty before us. We, too, emit such beauty when emerging from a time, even a season of struggle. Knowing that perseverance weighted in patience can produce a character fortified in soul muscle that was absent before is needed encouragement during the storm. Bright days are promised ahead, and we know and believe this but often need the reminder to settle the nerves when pain reaches our threshold and does not abate.

What are the sources of affliction? Well, there are many tributaries that can lead to a flood of troubling times, from health to wealth, from a gate of hate, or a cost in loss. Just looking around us can show colors of an adversary with limitless hues, blending in darkness to rob us of a joy not subject to any circumstance. But we hold on and do not sink in raging seas or fold in winds that could carry away all but a fortress.

King David knew of such circumstances, from personal to armies of raging battles. Yet in the midst, he would exclaim the fortress, the stronghold, the shield that was his refuge: "The Lord is my rock, my fortress and my deliverer; my God is my rock, in whom I take refuge, my shield and the horn of my salvation, my stronghold."[78]

Where do we go, and to whom do we seek to buffer the storm? Do we seek the power of the Holy Spirit that gives strength to weary souls? There is no one running from dutiful help on heaven's horizon. There are legions of wanting angels at our Lord's disposal, equipped and ready for battle in the unseen but all too real in the realm of life's existence.

"For Crying Out Loud" may be a section worth reviewing, for the Lord will always hear our cry; He is faithful and faithful always. His compassion is unmatched, and it is not a sympathy or an empathy but a solution that bathes us in an indescribable peace that floods our souls, and we are firmly planted in a foundation of love that weathers the storm. He is our stronghold, and we are safely guarded at all times and in all circumstances. Paul wrote to the Thessalonians when there was trouble in the church in Thessalonica to encourage a sure foundation of faith in overcoming: "Now may the Lord of peace Himself, continually grant you peace in every circumstance. The Lord be with you all."[79] It was true then, and it is true today. Our Lord is unchangeable, and He is with us in every circumstance. Throughout scripture, *God is with us* is a theme in every battle. The psalmist wrote, "The Lord Almighty is with us, the God of Jacob is our fortress."[80]

Moses wrote, "Do not be afraid or discouraged for the Lord your God is with you, He will never leave you nor forsake you."[81] And Isaiah served up the helping attitude, "Encourage the exhausted and strengthen the feeble."[82]

We are never alone, and even in the midst of battling our own storms, we can be that encouragement, that strength that will carry a brother or sister when they cannot walk. I see this encouragement, this strength in the hearts of the children at St. Jude Hospital. What a battle they face, and yet in the midst of that dire trauma, they instill the very hope that parents, family, and friends need, lifting them up from the troubling winds of an indiscriminate cancer.

And that is it, my friends. We have a purpose in the storm, and we are needed in the storm. We are beautiful feet that carry a message for all ages, and we say, *Look at us; we are more than conquerors.* "What, then, shall we say in response to these things? If God is with us, who can be against us?"[83] And I do not think it is too much of a stretch to say, *what* can be against us? Patient in affliction? Is that possible? "I can do everything through Him who gives me strength" is a good answer.[84]

THE HEALING

What is healing? And can there be perfect healing? That is, free from all disease, pain, hurt, or anything that has our attention that we do not want. From the very beginning, healing has been needed, physical and spiritual, and it will be needed for all time here on earth until a new earth and a new heaven is brought forth as promised. The prophets dealt with mountains of healing needs, many directly with the Lord's manifested presence with His audible voice, through dreams and visions, through His creation, by His Spirit, and more miraculously, by encountering God.

We know by His spoken word in scripture that Jesus performed many healings and volumes more that were not written of—the blind, the lame, and the deaf. Searching closely in these accounts reveals that the physical healing, though temporary, was always accompanied with the healing of the soul, a spiritual healing that would be eternal.

Many times in our lifespan, all of us will seek healing of some sort. There are no exceptions, and if we know this, we can prepare in advance for those times, for the request will be much the same: relief of a condition that has imperiled some ability from our normal way of living.

We search deep inside for answers that often elude understanding, and in some instances the irony of the perfecting is that suffering is required for the healing. How can it be that we should suffer to be perfected, or more correctly, *One* should suffer so that we would be made perfect? That is our Christian understanding:

perfected through suffering and death. Suffering becomes most meaningful with redeeming value—suffering to redeem. Made clean by the most valuable, life-giving blood. The ultimate healing that never again is needed. It is a cure-all remedy and has no bounds regarding a physical condition. It is the means by which we are brought to spiritual perfection in Christ. The body may wither, but the soul made new never fades and grows stronger with any and every suffering once in the saving hands of Jesus our Lord.

It is interesting that we are told that our Lord learned obedience from what He suffered. What form of obedience do we find in our suffering? Well, from a physical standpoint, we are quick to obey doctors and medical practitioners when they prescribe a remedy for our healing. And if we are suffering in a relationship, we listen to sources from friends to experts to reconcile differences and execute advice to heal deep wounds.

Expert advice is what we all seek, advice that is laser focused on the problem with the perfect remedy if we will only listen, trust, and obey, and that can come a number of different ways, as the Lord may choose. Our problems are not ours in a vacuum. There are connecting tentacles of which we may or may not know, and the Lord is directing that orchestra of many, playing His best concerto in symphonic acclaim. When we are suffering and in need of healing, it can be hard to look beyond our own needs. But when we do, we can find that in our suffering, we can be the very healing of another or others in need. When not my will but Thy will resonates in our hearts, a new horizon opens our eyes to see through a window of pain the rougher seas battering the hopes of others crying for help as well. These are the words of one suffering: "The Spirit Himself testifies with our spirit that we are children of God, and if children, heirs also, heirs of God and fellow heirs with Christ, if indeed we suffer with Him so that we may also be glorified with Him. For I consider that the sufferings of this present time are not worthy to be compared with the glory that is to be revealed to us."[85]

To be sure and not take the reflection out of context, Paul is reflecting on much suffering he has endured for the sake of Christ, which the Lord Himself spoke of to Ananias: "But the Lord said to him, 'Go, for he is a chosen vessel of Mine to bear My name before Gentiles, kings, and the children of Israel. For I will show him how many things he must suffer for My name's sake.'"[86] But the inference is that if we do the same comparison as Paul with the eternal glory to be revealed, there really is no comparison, and by acknowledging what awaits us in glory, we can endure, by strength of which we do not know, all temporal suffering, pain, and injury. It takes intentionality; it takes determination, pulling up the bootstraps, and even being able to thank the Lord in a most difficult time.

Healing runs deep into the bones and beyond. We can be sure to be healed, whether on earth or in waiting, for it shall come as promised. The new that is promised was declared by Peter on the island of Patmos, and his vivid vision is the proof of healing for those who are the Lord's. Peter describes our hope:

> *Then I saw a new heaven and a new earth, for the first heaven and the first earth passed away, and there is no longer any sea. And I saw the holy city, new Jerusalem, coming down out of heaven from God, prepared as a bride adorned for her husband. And I heard a loud voice from the throne, saying, "Behold, the tabernacle of God is among the people, and He will dwell among them, and they shall be His people, and God Himself will be among them, and He will wipe away every tear from their eyes; and there will no longer be any death; there will no longer be any mourning, or crying, or pain; the first things have passed away." (Rev. 21:1-4)*

Paul writes that "Faith is the assurance of things hoped for and the conviction of things not seen."[87] We have assurance and the conviction of a perfect healing at the Lord's discretion and timing. Oh, that it would come soon, but waiting on the Lord is a maturing in faith in which we become stronger and more than conquerors, overcoming what cannot hold us down. We have this healing guaranteed and provided even in advance.

Now the questions for the body of Christ: *Does it need healing? Do we need healing? Is there suffering in the body?* We only need to look around us and test our functioning. Are we acting in concert with each other, edifying the body and strengthening the core as believers. Are all things working together for the good, for God's kingdom here on earth? The simplest of answers is that much work needs to be done in spiritually exercising the body to build divine muscle that can move mountains. The key is to start exercising, and the manual for that is available at every level of humankind.

ONE BREAD, ONE BODY

Understanding this chapter's title is not grasped by the world because it is of the divine nature of God. It is wisdom that, apart from the Holy Spirit, is no wisdom at all. Paul introduced this concept as speaking to wise people: "I am speaking as to wise people. Judge for yourselves what I say. The cup of blessing that we give thanks for, is it not a sharing in the blood of Christ? The bread that we break, is it not a sharing in the body of Christ? Because there is one bread, we who are many are one body, for all of us share that one bread."[88]

So much to digest in the bread and wine we eat and drink. Paul exhorts that this exercise in faith should edify the body and build us up in Christ, not tear us apart. Yet in our church traditions, we find the dividing rod of terror and fear, the sword of doctrine in tradition, rather than the Sword of the Spirit, and all with the scriptural support necessary to keep His children estranged to the will of God. There is no doubt that the will of God is unity in the body. Defying that as the will of God will bring about a subtle heresy that is beyond words and resides in the pride of the heart.

So how do we share in this commanded unity (I don't believe that any true, faithful follower can substantiate it as a suggestion)? I believe it begins and ends at the cross. Yes, there is much leading to the cross that is foundational in our faith, and there is much after the cross as well. But the unity is found in the cross—the Body and Blood of Christ, broken and poured out for us that we may have life in partaking.

What measure of man can dilute or diminish the meaning of the cross? At the cross we find unity in all corners of the Christian church. Traditions cannot separate us, no matter how different, when we meet at the cross. We can only come empty to be filled to full measure in the fullness of Christ in faith at the cross, singing,

> *Alas, and did my Savior bleed*
> *and did my Sovereign die?*
> *Would He devote that sacred Head*
> *for such a worm as I?*
>
> *At the cross, at the cross,*
> *where I first saw the light*
> *and the burden of my heart rolled*
> *away, rolled away.*
> *It was there by faith,*
> *I received my sight*
> *and now I am happy all the day.*[89]

What tradition is found in that reckoning, or what can separate us from such love of God? Paul, in writing to all brothers and sisters in Christ, was convinced that the answer is *nothing,* and he expounded sufficiently to extol a conquering attitude in faith:

> *Who will separate us from the love of Christ? Will tribulation, or distress, or persecution, or famine, or nakedness, or peril, or sword? Just as it is written,*
>
> *"FOR YOUR SAKE WE ARE BEING PUT TO DEATH ALL DAY LONG;*
> *WE WERE CONSIDERED AS SHEEP TO BE SLAUGHTERED."*
>
> *But in all these things we overwhelmingly conquer through Him who loved us. For I am convinced that neither death, nor life, nor angels, nor principalities, nor things present, nor things to come, nor powers, nor height, nor depth, nor any other created thing, will be able to separate us from the love of God, which is in Christ Jesus our Lord. (Rom. 8:35-39)*

We see many fleshly separations, but true faith remains our stronghold. We are brothers and sisters in Christ, looking different, even acting different, but our profession of faith is found at the cross, and we are undivided; we are unified as one at the cross.

Paul, encouraging believers, wrote,

Therefore, since we have so great a cloud of witnesses surrounding us, let us also lay aside every encumbrance and the sin which so easily entangles us, and let us run with endurance the race that is set before us, fixing our eyes on Jesus, the author and perfecter of faith, who for the joy set before Him endured the cross, despising the shame, and has sat down at the right hand of the throne of God. For consider Him who has endured such hostility by sinners against Himself, so that you will not grow weary and lose heart. (Heb. 12:1-3)

So where do we fix our eyes? On the many denominational differences that can and unfortunately are used to divide us in the body of Christ? Or do we fix our eyes on the Author and Perfecter of our faith at the cross, where we became one in faith with the conquering words of our Lord: "It is finished" (John 19:30).

One bread, one body, one Lord.[90]

PART 3:
FOR THE LOVE OF GOD

John 3:16; Mark 12:30; John 15:17;
John 15:12; Ephesians 5:1-2

A CALL TO ACTION

It is amazing that through the ages responses to the same questions have the same differing answers that polarize listeners to a particular axiom and disassociate an otherwise union of thought. That is to say, there is nothing new under the sun regarding what, when, where, how, and why our perceptions, prejudices, and biases are formed.

"For the Love of God" is the title of this section (Part 3), and it invokes a basic premise regarding our Lord's foremost command in *love*. Scripture is clear regarding the love of God: He first loved us. What does that mean? We can put it into the practical reflection of a parent giving birth to a child—relating to us, the creation of God. That child has no concept of love, while the parents' love exists even before birth. The child then grows to know and love the parent. Out of that love comes the whole of a lifestyle that emulates this love in action through teaching and understanding, which formulates a character that runs deep into the bloodline.

Our Lord does not love because of who we are and what we do, and His life on earth demonstrated an amazing love that transcended human values and elicited followers that fell in love with Him. A profound act of selflessness and sacrifice was not made because of anything about us but because of everything about our Lord. Paul, one amazing follower of Christ, wrote in his letter to the church in Rome that it was while we were "yet sinners, Christ died for us" (Rom. 5:8). He later wrote to the Ephesians that works did not lead to a willing death as a propitiation of Jesus our Lord.

To not linger and get to the point, we are who we are, and we do what we do in response to His great love. What would we do for our greatest love? The Apostle John wrote, "Greater love has no one than this, that a person will lay down his life for his friends" (John 15:13). To bring Paul back into this dialogue, he continued his discourse to the Ephesians, writing, "Be imitators ["followers" is an accurate translation of the original Greek] of God therefore, as dearly beloved children and live a life of love, just as Christ loved us and gave Himself up as a fragrant offering and sacrifice to God" (Eph. 5:1-2). There is a lot there to unpack regarding a call to action in holiness. How is it that Christ loves us? There are many divine characteristics of His love, and I will mention three core postulates: forgiveness, mercy, and grace.

We well understand forgiveness because, if you are alive, you have experienced it in some fashion. It may be a dim shadow of the forgiveness we have in Christ Jesus, but it gives us a basic understanding that we are no longer subject to the disdain of another. Mercy is also understandable, knowing we do not get what we deserve when we have committed a grievance. Grace follows in understanding that we get what we do not deserve as a benefactor.

Loving as Christ loves does not come without understanding that what most often becomes a hurdle is in the execution of such love. We all have been there, is my estimation. So how can we forgive? How can we be expected to forgive? And mercy, mercy me. They are getting what they deserve for their untamed actions—an eye for an eye and a tooth for a tooth! And not only what they deserve, but I will inflict greater harm so that the message is clear: *Don't think about doing that again!* Grace may be the hardest in execution, for rewards are for those who earn them, deserve them, work for them, and excel above all others. Giving someone something they do not deserve tests the bounds of any affection and certainly love that needs to be unbridled.

To be sure, one has to have the whole of scripture, both Old and New Testaments, to grasp an understanding of that which is beyond understanding. Paul helps us in that understanding, writing to the Ephesians,

> *For this reason I kneel before the Father, from whom every family in heaven and on earth derives its name. I pray that out of His glorious riches He may strengthen you with power through his Spirit in your inner being, so that Christ may dwell in your hearts through faith. And I pray that you, being rooted and established in love, may have power, together with all the Lord's holy people, to grasp how wide and long and high and deep is the love of Christ, and to know this love that surpasses knowledge—that you may be filled to the measure of all the fullness of God. (Eph. 3:14-19)*

Filled to the measure of all the fullness of God. How can that be, but that it can be? Knowing this love and being this love is the measure and the fullness of God. His example was and is the fulfillment of the law and the prophets for all to see for all ages. He Himself, and only He, brings us to the fullness that is in God. We do not become God, but we are the fulfillment of His created purpose, made in the likeness of God. From the beginning, He revealed this purpose, and it is written, "So God created man in His own image, in the image of God He created him; male and female He created them."[91]

And so we search God's Word from beginning to end to know Him and His will for us as His creation in purpose and position and to love as He has loved us.

FOR HIS NAMESAKE

For many, finding purpose in life can be elusive, a day-to-day search that breaks out of daily routines that seem to be circles in rhythm, where the new day is just another day, repeating the yesterday except for infrequent planned interruptions, and they themselves become routine year to year.

So why do we do the things we do? What is our training that seems to have been left behind, other than basics we rationalize to contribute to our successes, or at least the position we have achieved that sustains us in our hope for the future?

Why do we do the things we do, and for who? Can we break it down into meaningful parts that justify our priorities? Aha! What is most important? What is least important? What is necessary; what is not? The psychology of this seems without bounds, with volumes written—many as theses to qualify a learned and earned diploma.

Because of the pace of life these days, it is probable that most of us do not ponder these explorative questions and simply accept that we have lived another day. Of course, we, in some fashion, plan our days, often in advance—a dynamic reactionary planning that responds to needs we are responsible for. It is possible that others plan our days more than we, ourselves, do, which is an excellent segway to elicit a call to the master planner of all time.

Our Lord spoke to the prophet Jeremiah and said, "For I know the plans I have for you,' declares the Lord, 'plans to prosper you and not to harm you, plans to give you hope and a future.'"[92] This was a message to Jeremiah after the nation of Israel had been banished to Babylon because of their rejection of God and His ways, pursuing their own ways. Can it be that God has a plan for us? Can it be to prosper and not to harm us? For the Israelites, it may have sounded grossly rhetorical given their current circumstances.

But when is it that we must be most courageous in hope and search for deeper meanings to direct our lives? The answer to the questions above ("Can it be?") is, *Yes!* Yes, it can. There is a plan for each and every one of us. Given, it has wide latitude, I think mostly for our enjoyment and exercise of the rich freedoms we are given in Christ. Some of us have prayed about moves we have made, jobs we have taken, and spouses we have married, seeking the Lord's direction and approval. We reach a threshold of cognitive dissonance and look for confirmations, and a decision is made that has significant impact for the future. The latitude our Lord gives, I think, can be summed up in a couple of scriptural truths: "Whatever you do, work at it with all of your heart as working for the Lord, not for man, since you know that you will receive an inheritance from the Lord as a reward. It is the Lord Christ you are serving."[93] This message that Paul delivered to the Colossians was not to ministers, it was not to priests, it was not to those who served in the church alone; it was to all believers regardless of their vocation.

I remember a pastor I met while serving in ministry in Myrtle Beach. When our children were young, we were campers. I had always been a camper growing up—a *tent* camper. But to include my wife in these adventures, I had to convert my tent mentality to a thirty-six-foot metal home on wheels with air conditioning and most of the conveniences we had back home. (I want to make sure that, reading this, you would not think I was forcing hardship on my wife for things that bring me enjoyment. But back to the pastor.) It was a Sunday morning worship service on the beach, and the sun was rising (I know, what hardship?). I was talking with the pastor before the service on the subject of knowing and doing the Lord's will. He shared with me a moment he had with his wife in the trailer they lived in. It was a Saturday morning, and he was relaxing on the couch (probably reviewing notes for his sermon) while his wife vacuumed. He said he thought he was paying her a compliment in thanksgiving when he said to her, "I am so blessed with a wife that does these things for me in our household with such excellence." He was caught just a bit off guard when she responded, "You think I do these things for you? I do them for the Lord."

At first, we may smile a bit or chuckle, but her response was deeply rooted in motive, and whatever she did, she did to please the Lord; it was her best, always. He shared this so that we do not get caught so much in the anxiety of what to do but get caught up in *why* we are doing it and *for whom.*

Another truth was shared by Paul to the Corinthians because of requirements of the Tora and stipulations about what one could or could not eat or drink:

> *All things are permitted, but not all things are of benefit. All things are permitted, but not all things build people up. No one is to seek his own good, but rather that of his neighbor. (1 Cor. 10:23-24)*

> *Now by "conscience" I do not mean your own, but the other person's; for why is my freedom judged by another's conscience? If I partake with thankfulness, why am I slandered about that for which I give thanks? Therefore, whether you eat or drink, or whatever you do, do all things for the glory of God. (1 Cor. 10:29-31)*

What is the message that was and is delivered even for us? Search for the motive; this can often boil down to only one or two things: our glory or the glory of God.

So why do we do the things we do, and for whom? For our namesake or our Lord's? We know the Lord does things for His namesake that often deliver us from His wrath. The prophet

Isaiah penned these words: "For the sake of My name I delay My wrath, and for My praise I restrain it for you in order not to cut you off. Behold, I have refined you, but not as silver; I have tested you in the furnace of affliction, for My own sake, for My own sake, I will act; For how can My name be profaned? And I will not give My glory to another."[94]

For His namesake, the Lord acts. For His namesake, we too should act.

ANGELS ATTENDING

Ever feel alone? I believe that most everyone has, at some point in their lives, if only for a moment, and then a convicted heart lets us know that we are never alone. There has been much written about God's army of angels, and this is not a discourse on the justification of angels and their actions. We do know what we are told and that God does give angels charge over us. What that understanding is can be vague because we know little about the daily interactions between the seen and unseen. The movie *It's a Wonderful Life*, starring Jimmy Stewart, depicts a novel relationship of such with a resulting good triumphing over evil.

The attention and responsibility given to angels is the Lord's privilege, and we can be sure that it is purposed in the triumph of the goodness of God. The psalmist wrote, "If you say, 'The Lord is my refuge,' and you make the Most High your dwelling, no harm will overtake you, no disaster will come near your tent. For he will command his angels concerning you to guard you in all your ways. They will lift you up in their hands, so that you will not strike your foot against a stone" (Ps. 91:9-12). This is not hyperbole but the very truths that reveal a loving God, who has our most intimate interests fully at heart, with His kingdom ready at our side in all our ways so that we can stand and not fall. Wow! Have you ever thought about the many of God's servants who have been disposed to us and are with us? If God is for us, who can come against us?

And we know that in all things God works for the good of those who love him, who have been called according to his purpose. For those God foreknew he also predestined to be conformed to the image of his Son, that he might be the firstborn among many brothers and sisters. And those he predestined, he also called; those he called, he also justified; those he justified, he also glorified. What, then, shall we say in response to these things? If God is for us, who can be against us? He who did not spare his own Son, but gave him up for us all— how will he not also, along with him, graciously give us all things? Who will bring any charge against those whom God has chosen? It is God who justifies. Who then is the one who condemns? No one. Christ Jesus who died—more than that, who was raised to life—is at the right hand of God and is also interceding for us. (Rom. 8:28-34)

Angels guarding us in all our ways, and a great advocate, the Lord Himself, interceding for us. What more can we ask? What more can we need? "His divine power gives us everything we need for life and godliness through our knowledge of Him, who called us by His own glory and goodness."[95]

There really is not much more to be written here except to exclaim that our life's battle array is supported such that we are more than conquerors in all these things through Him who loved us. There is more to the seen that is unseen, but not unknown, for it has been revealed to us. New strength finds its way into our bones when we are cognizant of the spiritual resources that are not passive but active for our every need. That is the key. Are we always aware of our angel friends and the unceasing intercession of our Lord? I believe that when we are encouraged to pray unceasingly, that is the avenue of plenty—fruit that is seen and expressed in love, joy, peace, patience, kindness, goodness, faithfulness, gentleness, and self-control. A well-orbed life where the circle is endlessly surrounding the circumstances we find ourselves in each and every day.

It is a 24/7 attention we have, never waning and fully readied for our good. To reflect the psalmist in song (Ps. 18:3),

> *I will call upon the LORD, who is worthy to be praised,*
> *And I am saved from my enemies.*[96]

Are we taking full advantage of our Lord's promises? If not, why not? We will know Him intimately when we incorporate those promises into our daily lives and call upon Him at all times. His angels are always at the ready.

INSTRUMENT OF LOVE

There is only one purpose of an instrument, and that is to be used by the one who knows how to use it. One that knows how it was created and for what purpose. Unused instruments have no value regarding their purpose. Some may become items valuable to a collector, but not valuable in their use per se.

An instrument may open a channel allowing the creation of something new that was never before. A vocalist is an instrument of music and, when singing, fills a room that was vacant of pleasant sound. An orchestra is filled with different instruments used in concert to produce a symphony of music that could not be produced by one alone.

There are instruments used to diagnose sickness and its source for remedy. There are instruments that probe, that measure, that warn, that record, that are used to move things, that secure and protect things. Instruments are made and used for the benefit of the user and the intended audience or subjects.

The definition of an instrument is vast in its understanding, with the common inference in secular notions:

1. a tool or implement, especially one for delicate or scientific work: "a surgical instrument"

   Synonyms: implement, tool, utensil, device, apparatus, contrivance, gadget, contraption, appliance, mechanism

2. a measuring device used to gauge the level, position, speed, etc. of something, especially a motor vehicle or aircraft: "a

new instrument for measuring ozone levels"

Synonyms: gauge, meter, measure, indicator, dial, display, measuring device

3. an object or device for producing musical sounds: "a percussion instrument"

4. a formal document, especially a legal one: "execution involves signature and unconditional delivery of the instrument"

VERB

instrument

equip (something) with measuring instruments: "engineers have instrumented rockets to study the upper atmosphere"

ORIGIN

Middle English: from Old French, or from Latin *instrumentum,* "equipment, implement," from the verb *instruere,* "construct, equip."[97]

The origin is interesting, being a derivative from the root action verb *construct* or *equip*. It gives the notion that an instrument is not without ownership. There has to be a making, a construction equipped for a genuine purpose. If there is creation, if there is purpose, there is an instrument for that purpose to be used as designed, and the execution is in the rightful use that benefits its surroundings.

It is not difficult to see ourselves as a created instrument of our God—a God where everything in His creation basket is designed in concert for a purpose: His purpose. That purpose is revealed in His spoken word and is relatable to our understanding of what an instrument is and does as demonstrated above. Every instrument does not act on its own. There are commands given humanly, scientifically, and even spiritually for the transcendent understanding for our lives. We could review all of these, or we can simply sum up the Creator's commands as He, the Creator, did. He was asked what the greatest of His commands was:

> *"Teacher, which is the greatest commandment in the Law?" Jesus replied: "Love the Lord your God with all your heart and with all your soul and with all your mind. This is the first and greatest commandment. And the second is like it: Love your neighbor as yourself. All the Law and the Prophets hang on these two commandments." (Matt. 22:36-40)*

That being the greatest of commands to a created instrument would relegate us as believers to being an instrument of love, constructed and equipped to be such—signaling, probing, measuring, recording, warning, securing, and protecting, for His benefit, for His good pleasure, and for our good and the good of all of His church, the body of many instruments working in concert for His glory and His honor, for He is worthy as Creator, Producer, Sustainer, and Owner.

Do we think of ourselves as instruments of love? And how does that get played through us? Do we even know what love is? The secularists define it as a deep affection or to like and enjoy very much. A strong and positive emotional and mental state, usually entertaining a sexual inference. What it doesn't conclude is that love, true love, is beyond understanding. The married can ask their spouse, "Why do you love me?" The answer (maybe smiling), "I don't know," may be in jest, but that really is the right answer because anything beyond human understanding is beyond knowing. Some may begin listing attributes or things that are done for the sake of the other, but as well-meaning as they may be, they fall short of true love that is unexplainable.

Our Lord is most sincere about knowing if we love Him, and we see the intensity of that in His questioning Peter at breakfast:

> *When they had finished eating, Jesus said to Simon Peter, "Simon son of John, do you love me more than these?"*
>
> *"Yes, Lord," he said, "you know that I love you."*
>
> *Jesus said, "Feed my lambs."*

> *Again Jesus said, "Simon son of John, do you love me?"*
> *He answered, "Yes, Lord, you know that I love you."*
> *Jesus said, "Take care of my sheep." The third time he said to him, "Simon son of John, do you love me?" Peter was hurt because Jesus asked him the third time, "Do you love me?" He said, "Lord, you know all things; you know that I love you." Jesus said, "Feed my sheep."*
> *(John 21:15-17)*

Some theologians refer to that account as a reinstatement of Peter in relationship because of his thrice denial of Jesus in the courtyard outside of the high priest's house. Personally, I do not believe that when Peter denied Jesus that it was a denial of His love for Him, and reinstatement may miss the mark in the true motive of Jesus questioning him. Note that after each response, there are instructions by Jesus that are ultimately followed and fulfilled by Peter. Jesus is directing Peter's love in a practical and executable demonstration of His love. Sometimes, I'm convinced we feel we are demonstrating our love, but if we are listening to God whom we love, we will know what is expected for proof.

Notice also the different Greek words that are used in the exchange. Jesus first uses the word *agape*: the Greek derivation meaning "unconditional love." Peter responded with *phileo*: the Greek derivation meaning "a brotherly, friendship type of love." The third time Jesus uses the same term as Peter, *phileo*, and Peter responds in kind with *phileo*.

Some propose that Jesus is trying to move Peter from a brotherly love to a higher-level unconditional love. What I would propose is that Jesus is encompassing the broad spectrum of what love entails. Jesus has already called the disciples "friends," including Peter. This would be an acknowledgment that they knew their Master and His business—Jesus' purpose that would be passed to them—fulfilling the Father's will to bring His people back into relationship to the praise and glory of His name.

> *Early in the morning, Jesus stood on the shore, but the disciples did not realize that it was Jesus. He called out to them, "Friends, haven't you any fish?" (John 21:4-5)*

> *"I no longer call you servants, because a servant does not know his master's business. Instead, I have called you friends, for everything that I learned from my Father I have made known to you." (John 15:15)*

I believe that we are able to see the intentionality of Jesus driving the point of unconditional love that is required in sacrifice as friends, knowing in purpose what He desires in obedience, demonstrating the love that makes the relationship real and not a façade of emotions.

Peter, do you love me unconditionally? Do this. Peter, is your love such that you know my purpose in you? Do this. Yes, Peter, I confirm your friendship in knowing me and my purpose in you; do it.

I think this is plausible in understanding the exchange for our purpose as well because the Lord wants to see the same orb of understanding in us. Do we truly love Jesus? I once asked a pastor in exchange, "Do you love Jesus?" I will always remember his response: "I have a lot of things that are wrong with me, but oh, how I love Jesus!" I could feel the genuineness in his response beyond emotion, and it was exhilarating just to be a part of such an acknowledgment that transcended the moment physically—unexplainable and beyond understanding—but knowing such love that can be expressed in demonstrated service and sacrifice.

That's it, a simple instrument of love being played out in daily life that is exhilarating not only to the one who loves but to all who are brought along the path of the faithful. Who am I? I'm hoping my identity is as simple as an *instrument of love.*

A VOICE IN THE DESERT

Do you hear voices? Your first inclination and response might be that you have gone a bit off the pier, so to speak. Hallucination might be the reference, but if you have a conscience (you do), something is internally challenging you to listen, whether you do or not. So where does that come from? It has been said in psychology terms that it is a cognitive process that elicits emotion and rational associations based on an individual's moral philosophy or value system, meaning that the source can be just about anything—realistically a moving target when trying to pinpoint whatever is causing the interaction. That is a rather worldly reference by every means, for it evades considering beyond existential thought or accepting mystical reality.

When we consider the truths that are taught in biblical exposition, we know that God's Holy Spirit is the source of all consciousness, even in nonbelievers, though He does not reside within them. And a voice that is heard often brings revelation of the presence of God to realization. He is a protector of His name and His ways, reminding us of who He is. The right way He promotes will stir the faintest in faith. I believe He gives special attention to His holiness in all levels of our walk in faith.

Moses, one of His called to lead His people, spent forty days and nights in the desert as a training ground, and at one particular time an epiphany of epiphanies struck him in bewilderment. The account of the burning bush is beyond human explanation in science, as an eternal fire was upon a bush that would garner his attention, and as he would approach, a voice from the bush would be heard saying, "Do not come near here; remove your sandals from your feet, for the place on which you are standing is holy ground."[98] We all are pretty familiar with desert ground. It is probably not a place you would choose to go for a vacation retreat. It is hot in the daytime and cold at night. The only water found may be merely a mirage. And there are unholy creatures like snakes and scorpions and bugs that like human flesh. So the question is, what in the world (nothing in the world) would turn desert ground into holy ground but the presence of the Holy One who makes all things holy at His command? God reveals Himself to Moses, and in response, Moses "hid his face, for he was afraid to look at God."[99]

A voice is heard, and God is now speaking. Have we heard His voice from the midst of the fire? We may not experience such an event in our lives, but we know that God's character and desires can be whispered in our ears: "What I tell you in the darkness, tell in the light; and what you hear whispered in your ear, proclaim on the housetops."[100]

Elijah's mountain experience would also find the uniqueness and selectivity of a God who says "I Am" regarding how and where He will reveal Himself.

> *The LORD said, "Go out and stand on the mountain in the presence of the LORD, for the LORD is about to pass by." Then a great and powerful wind tore the mountains apart and shattered the rocks before the LORD, but the LORD was not in the wind. After the wind there was an earthquake, but the LORD was not in the earthquake. After the earthquake came a fire, but the LORD was not in the fire. And after the fire came a gentle whisper. When Elijah heard it, he pulled his cloak over his face and went out and stood at the mouth of the cave. (1 Kings 19:11-13)*

God would constantly tell His people throughout the ages, *If only you will listen obediently to the voice of the Lord your God, to follow carefully all this commandment which I am commanding you today.* And yes, He is still telling His people today. It may or may not be pleasing to the ear what we hear, but an obedient heart will listen and take heed. Jeremiah and other contemporaries of his time understood this as recorded in the book of his name: "Whether it is pleasant or unpleasant, we will listen to the voice of the Lord our God to whom we are sending you, so that it may go well for us when we listen to the voice of the Lord our God."[101]

Whether it is a voice in desert times, troubling times, flourishing times, or just ordinary times, it is a voice that I submit everyone hears, and the essence of hearing or not is in the acceptance or rejection and obedience or disobedience to execute the will of God. A voice calling in the desert is a voice worth listening to, for we can find the holiness of God wherever we are and wherever we go.

BY THE SEA

By the beautiful sea! What is it about the sea that draws us almost enchantingly to its beauty? The poetry that unfolds, the dreams that capture our minds to wander along the shores. We visualize the enchantment and see the sunrises and sunsets, ships on the horizon, and children frolicking in the lapping waves. We catch a glimpse of fishermen waiting for that one catch they can brag on with friends listening in awe.

We know virtually all that the sea contains and beckons to its waters and its beaches. Those who are novices to its shores and those who know every nuance of its secrets. All come to visit, and many come to live and fill their days with everything it has to offer. There is breakfast at sunrise, lunch at noonday calm, and dinner at sunset with joy upon joy—it is an enjoyment of postcard scenes to write home about.

But there is also the unruly that catches even the most experienced sea-weathering person off guard, and fear seeps into the mind from the raging of the waves, casting bows over the largest vessels made to safely traverse the oceans. Though man has never tamed the seas, the seas have tamed many a man. That might be a coined saying with heartfelt meaning, but it would need to be qualified because there was one Man who tamed the seas just by speaking: our Lord, Jesus Christ, who can speak to His creation from the mountains to the seas and everything in between, and they have no choice but to respond in obedience.

Every experience imaginable brought our Lord's attention for the purpose of revealing Himself and His authority over His creation. Remember the night His disciples had pushed out to sea, set for the other side, when suddenly, as the account is recorded, a fierce storm came up to where there was great fear in all except for Jesus, who was sleeping in the stern:

> *That day when evening came, he said to his disciples, "Let us go over to the other side." Leaving the crowd behind, they took him along, just as he was, in the boat. There were also other boats with him. A furious squall came up, and the waves broke over the boat, so that it was nearly swamped. Jesus was in the stern, sleeping on a cushion. The disciples woke him and said to him, "Teacher, don't you care if we drown?"*
>
> *He got up, rebuked the wind and said to the waves, "Quiet! Be still!" Then the wind died down and it was completely calm. He said to his*

> *disciples, "Why are you so afraid? Do you still have no faith?" They were terrified and asked each other, "Who is this? Even the wind and the waves obey him!" (Mark 4:35-41)*

They ask the question that has been asked from the beginning of time and continues to be asked: "Who is this?" And we know His account with Peter: "Who do they say that I am? Who do you say that I am?" Who do we say that He is?

The best question to ask is, *Who does He say that He is?* The religious leaders of His day asked Him if He was the Son of God, and He responded, "Yes, I am."[102] We have digressed slightly but importantly to establish who this is that has authority to command the sea. He is either who He says He is, or He is a liar; there is no account of Him, scripturally or historically, where He is anything but the truth. Not just in storms does He have authority, but whenever there is purpose in His will to expose truth and to draw His people closer to Him.

There was such an account to draw His disciples close to Him after His resurrection in an appearance by the Sea of Galilee.[103] It was by the sea that He invited them to breakfast, and we find that oracle of instructional love. Can you imagine such an invitation where He calls you by His side? None of the disciples dared ask him, "Who are You?" They knew it was the Lord.

I am convinced that when He invites you to come alongside, maybe not by the sea but wherever you are, He will be with that continual feeding of His love, and you will know that it is the Lord.

By the sea, by the beautiful sea . . . we can only imagine until faith becomes sight, and we see Him face to face. No imagination can provide the immeasurable joy that will be experienced at that homecoming.

32

THE WAY

The way that leads to life is narrow (Matt. 7:13-14)

Instructed in the way of the Lord; the way of God (Acts 18:24-25)

Proclaim to you the way of the Lord (Acts 16:17)

Jesus said, "I Am the Way, the Truth and the Life" (John 14:6)

In the book of Acts, "The Way" is the most widely known name for the early Christian church. We find in Saul's zealous desire in persecuting believers, followers of Jesus as risen Lord, threats and even murder schemes to terminate such belief:

> *Now Saul, still breathing threats and murder against the disciples of the Lord, went to the high priest, and asked for letters from him to the synagogues at Damascus, so that if he found any belonging to the Way, both men and women, he might bring them bound to Jerusalem. (Acts 9:1-2)*

> *Hardened and disobedient people spoke evil about the Way. (Acts 19:8-9)*

> *About that time there occurred no small disturbance concerning the way. (Acts 19:23)*

> *The disturbance about the Way, the early church body of believers, led to a near riot in Ephesus. (Acts 19:23-41)*

We know of Saul's conversion and transformation that led to truth being revealed for a change that would transpose persecution into preservation, and his new understanding in revelation would lead his efforts in preservation to persecution he knew so well as promoter of such. He would be brought under Roman custody to Caesarea, where he testified before Felix, the governor.

> *"This I admit to you, that according to the Way which they call a sect, I do serve the God of our fathers, believing everything that is in accordance with the Law and that is written in the Prophets." (Acts 24:14)*

"The Way" is mentioned several times in Acts, while the name "Christian" is mentioned three times in the entire New Testament (Acts 11:26; 26:28; 1 Pet. 4:16). That is not to say one is more important than the other or that one is preferred over the other. It is just to reference, historically, that the early church was identified as "The Way." Personally, in today's world, conformity by many are churches in name. I like the earliest biblical reference to believers in fellowship and to the biblical reference of the way that leads to a person who stands alone as the head of the church:

> *He is the image of the invisible God, the firstborn of all creation: for by Him all things were created, both in the heavens and on earth, visible and invisible, whether thrones, or dominions, or rulers, or authorities—all things have been created through Him and for Him. He is before all things, and in Him all things hold together. He is also the head of the body, the church; and He is the beginning, the firstborn from the dead, so that He Himself will come to have first place in everything. For it was the Father's good pleasure for all the fullness to dwell in Him, and through Him to reconcile all things to Himself, whether things on earth or things in heaven, having*

> *made peace through the blood of His cross. (Col. 1:18-20)*

He is of authority, and the true body functions according to His will. His Word prevails in all things. There is no adding or deleting for risk of going astray on a way that seems right to a man but leads to death.

Conformity to the world may seem like a fair way to deal with issues of the day, but nowhere is our Lord committed to fairness in our typical understanding. What He says He is committed to and provides a way for is justice, for He is a just God that never changes. I think of Uzzah, when he reached out and took hold of the Arc of the Covenant, for it was nearly upset on the cart by the oxen. Right there the Lord's burning anger and resulting wrath was administered immediately in his death. Our first reaction? How in the world does that make sense? The answer is, in the world, it doesn't. But in God's righteousness, in God's holiness, in the reverence due Him based on what He reveals to us in His Way, it makes every bit of sense.

Even "David became angry because of the Lord's outburst against Uzzah" (2 Sam. 6:8). You can imagine, how is this fair in life? David had directed Uzzah and Ahio and instructed them on moving the Arc of the Covenant, but his instruction, his method, was not according to God's instruction and method.

The holiness of God is very serious; it is absolute to those who claim to serve Him and acknowledge His rule. It is *His Way or the highway,* would be an appropriate description, though even that thought would raise the hair on the prideful in heart. Who died and made Him King? He did! And He said, "I Am The Way, The Truth, and The Life. No one comes to the Father, but through Me."[104]

33

CAST ME NOT

The mercies of God are central to who He is, and they are new every morning, constantly revealing a love that captures hearts so distant that the seemingly impossible becomes possible.

The psalmist knew this God of abundant mercy and unfathomable love and records the humble and prayerful brokenness that is the sacrifice that God will not despise:[105]

> *Have mercy on me, O God,*
> *according to your steadfast love;*
> *according to your abundant mercy*
> *blot out my transgressions.*
> *Wash me thoroughly from my iniquity,*
> *and cleanse me from my sin!*
> *(Ps. 51:1-2)*

This mercy, in simple terms, is substitutionary; we don't get what we deserve in penalty for what is in our own nature, to transgress what God has set before us for life in godliness. We only need to pause and take inventory of actions that are not of long ago, and we, too, will repeat the plea that resonates in the halls of justice.

Substitutionary is quite accurate to expand the horizon of thought to just what could be that replacement. There is no legally generated substitution in written law. There is no money exchange, though there is payment. The remarkable propitiation is that it is a person in sacrifice of all that is all in life, and it is not just any person that can make that sacrifice in substitution, but only one: the Son of God. From the beginning, He was planned to be sent by the Father and be among those He would save from the tyranny of their sinful nature that holds captive one's own way. He would cause a cosmic collision at the cross, a collision of justice and grace from the mercy that was shed on those He loved.

Forgiveness, mercy, and grace, before judgment of a just God, and found in the fellowship of mankind, is necessary for iron to sharpen iron in our walk of faith. The words of the psalmist above are the words that have frequented our prayers. This writer was a man not far from God but with a distant heart. He was near to God, enabling him to recognize God for who He is and what He can do, and realizing who he, the psalmist, was and what he needed.

Knowing God will bring us to that realization of just who we are. I do not believe that apart from truly knowing God, we can really know who we are because it is God who knows our innermost thoughts. He knew us before we were knit in the womb, and He alone can reveal to us who we really are. Then, a most amazing thing happens: He increases, and we decrease to where a Master takes hold of our lives, and we are freed from the very things that hold us captive in our own way. This freedom enables us to say "no" to our very selves, to the very things we desire that are meaningless to our God.

When we begin to know ourselves, we recognize things about us that often lie below the surface, unseen and most often unknown. The psalmist continues his self-examination:

> *For I know my transgressions;*
> *And my sin is ever before me.*
> *Against Thee, Thee only, have I sinned,*
> *And done that which is evil in thy sight;*
> *That thou mayest be justified when thou speakest,*
> *And be clear when Thou judgest.*
> *(Ps. 51:3-4)*

I am sure we can identify with the secret offense that has not caught the awareness of anyone, and we think that we have gotten away with something. This becomes an inner awareness that, when convicted as the psalmist, we discover, and the only thing we have "gotten away with" is judgment before man—but not judgment itself. For we are seen always in the light of who we are. Nothing is unseen before our God, and we stand naked in words, thoughts, and actions, unclothed and exposed to the openness of the heart. "Against Thee, Thee only, have I sinned" is an admission of guilt that transposes the earthly man to a walking, spiritual being that weighs the consequences with admission before a God of forgiveness, mercy, and grace.

> *Behold, Thou desirest truth in the inward parts;*
> *And in the hidden part thou wilt make me to know wisdom.*
> *Purify me with hyssop, and I shall be clean;*
> *Wash me, and I shall be whiter than snow. (Ps. 51:6-7)*

Though what is seen in us on the outside is important, of utmost importance is what is transpiring within us, and that is where our God is searching. A heart that is completely His is what He searches for throughout mankind, throughout His creation, to strongly support, and when He finds such a heart, He begins to mold us in His image to where we are most like Him, and our identity is not found in the conformity of the world but in the presence of a living God, and our prayer becomes like the psalmist:

> *Create in me a clean heart, O God;*
> *And renew a right spirit within me.*
> *Cast me not away from thy presence;*
> *And take not Thy Holy Spirit from me. (Ps. 51:10-11)*

The presence of our God, a holy God, is what makes us holy because He is holy, and His righteousness prevails in hearts that recognize who He is and who we have become.

Cast me not, O God, that I may walk always in the Spirt, alive in the Spirit, living in the Spirit. Cast me not.

34

THE BOUNTY

Oh, the bounty of the Lord! "He gives us everything we need for life and godliness through our knowledge of Him who called us by His own glory and grace" (2 Pet. 1:3). Does our Lord often give us more than even we could ask for? That is my experience, and yes, often *more than we could ever ask for,* would be an honest answer. Should we be given what we ask for might never gain the rich blessings that He fully intends for us. And yes, those certainly include material blessings, though not by themselves are we thankful, for many of those pass away and are just fond memories from a gracious God we love.

The Israelites were recipients of such bounty as a people and as a nation. Most prominent might be the period of their restoration—both the northern and southern kingdom after the Lord brought them back out of captivity in Babylon. Jeremiah records the pinnacle of the return to God's chosen place for His sanctuary, the height of Zion:

> *"They will come and shout for joy on the height of Zion, and they will be radiant over the bounty of the Lord. Over the grain and the new wine and the oil, and over the young of the flock and the herd; and their life will be like a watered garden, and they will never languish again." (Jer. 31:12)*

Land that will produce much was given for their pleasure. Not just in what the land gave from its rich resources, but what multiplied through vibrant herds that fed the many. Material blessings for their life needs on earth, satisfying them with the Lord's goodness—thus, He said.

It is amazing how much more the Lord gives than what we would ask for. Those of us who are parents give gifts our children do not ask for, even beyond their needs, simply because of our love for them. Their excitement in receiving them and their thanksgiving is something that is most pleasant and honorable in seeing and receiving. How much more He says He is than what we can even know:

> *"Which of you, if your son asks for bread, will give him a stone? Or if he asks for a fish, will give him a snake? If you, then, though you are evil, know how to give good gifts to your children, how much more will your Father in heaven give good gifts to those who ask him! So in everything, do to others what you would have them do to you, for this sums up the Law and the Prophets." (Matt. 7:9-12)*

There it is again, the principle of multiplication: "So in everything." We are to multiply these good gifts as the Lord Himself has shown us, finding and blessing beneficiaries for the Lord, not for our sake but for His namesake.

Throughout scripture it is shown how God cares for His people, knowing their needs more than they themselves, and provides for them as Jehovah Jireh. The songwriter of "There Shall Be Showers of Blessing" depicts a washing in the many blessings of the Lord.[106] The Lord showers us with blessings and we bathe in the goodness of the Lord, His bounty and bountiful provision. And then there is the most bountiful provision of all: our salvation. Material to our lives forever, eternally. That is the languish that will never be again. Nothing is able to separate us from the love of God, and we will enjoy Him forever. What bounty is this that we have this boundless love? Crowned with His righteousness, the bounty is set before us, and we feast on the goodness of the Lord abundantly flowing, cascading like a fountain filled with blood, and beneath that flood of washing waters not a guilty stain remains.

The battle of all time was fought and won, and we bring the bounty into our storehouse that spills out into the world's avenues to the praise and glory of Jehovah Jireh, the Great I Am, for us, and He writes of us in the Book of the Lamb. There is a bounty upon our heads, and it is the bounty of the Lord.

35

BOILING OVER

I am fairly confident that we seldom think of God's presence as something boiling over, but we do know that fire has an important role in His plans and is important to our understanding.

Fire and sacrifice seem to go hand in hand to refine us to be able to recognize God Almighty as the One and true God, knowing there is no other. We find an amazing account of this demonstration where Elijah challenges King Ahab and more than eight hundred fifty false prophets, gathering them at Mount Carmel to determine who is God and who isn't.

"Now therefore send and gather all Israel to me at Mount Carmel, and the 450 prophets of Baal and the 400 prophets of Asherah, who eat at Jezebel's table."

So Ahab sent to all the people of Israel and gathered the prophets together at Mount Carmel. And Elijah came near to all the people and said, "How long will you go limping between two different opinions? If the LORD is God, follow him; but if Baal, then follow him." And the people did not answer him a word. Then Elijah said to the people, "I, even I only, am left a prophet of the LORD, but Baal's prophets are 450 men. Let two bulls be given to us, and let them choose one bull for themselves and cut it in pieces and lay it on the wood, but put no fire to it. And I will prepare the other bull and lay it on the wood

> *and put no fire to it. And you call upon the name of your god, and I will call upon the name of the LORD, and the God who answers by fire, he is God." (1 Kings 18:19-24)*

Through a series of attempts by the prophets of Baal to call on their god to respond to the challenge, and Elijah's constant disparaging and mocking them in defeat, we find that against all laws of science and human intellect, the God who is God responds to a water-soaked altar with trenched water surrounding, with fire consuming the offering and everything with it. Water not only boiled over, but it was licked out of being.

> *Then the fire of the Lord fell and consumed the burnt offering and the wood and the stones and the dust, and licked up the water that was in the trench. And when all the people saw it, they fell on their faces and said, "The Lord, he is God; the Lord, he is God." (1 Kings 18:38-39)*

Fire and water do render a reference to sacrifice and provision biblically in the Old Testament, with instructions to the people and the priests of what is required at the altar before the Lord. Another account was when the Lord revealed to Elijah that Elisha would be the prophet in his place, and when he went and found him, Elisha responded by sacrificing, not leaving anything behind to return to.

> *And he returned from following him and took the yoke of oxen and sacrificed them and boiled their flesh with the yokes of the oxen and gave it to the people, and they ate. (1 Kings 19:21)*

Isaiah penned a prayer for mercy and help and called, what I think was desperately, upon the Lord to come, acknowledging the greatness, the oneness of our God in whom there is no equal:

> *Oh, that You would rend the heavens and come down, that the mountains might quake at Your presence. As*

fire kindles the brushwood, as fire causes water to boil—to make Your name known to Your adversaries, that the nations may tremble at your presence! When You did awesome things which we did not expect, You came down, the mountains quaked in Your presence. From days of old they have not heard or perceived by ear, nor has the eye seen a God besides You, who acts on behalf of the one who waits for Him. (Isa. 64:1-4)

Fire is the operative cause in allegory, and we can imagine the graduating sequence of something starting almost unnoticeable and growing to where things seem out of control. I have witnessed boiling water cascading over the pot onto the stove when distracted long enough for it to control its own destiny. My wife occasionally asks me to start the spaghetti or prepare some hard-boiled eggs for the tuna salad, and in both instances, I have achieved the escape act of water to help her understand that she's the cook!

When the Lord is asked to come, He doesn't just tiptoe through the tulips. He doesn't casually brush by our side and say, "I'm here." We know of His entrance MO, and it is usually accompanied by events that are not describable and cause a rightful fear of reverence that no other can command. That said, we do know that when the Son of God arrived on earth, it was like a lamb, and without much earthly fanfare. But oh, how the heavens were rejoicing with unimaginable star guidance, bringing humble adoration with gifts that would tell more than eyes could see or minds conceive.

We know also that this same and only Son of God who left the earth in a manner that would leave the most renowned scientists declaring it impossible, will come back the same way, but with a host of heavenly ones that will rend the heavens and cause the mountains to quake. The Lamb who was always a Lion, and the Lion who was always a Lamb, will reveal the judgment cloak adorned with authority to bring an end to the old that will pass away and bring a new heaven and a new earth where righteousness will be the order of every day.

That end is what is promised in boiling over from fire that will melt away every form of the universe with a refining that separates and eradicates evil from existence. We can visualize but a shadow of what that will be like.

36

IS HE COMING?

Yes, the Lord is coming again, is the quick and accurate response to a question that is most rhetorical! It is a promise; it is His promise, and throughout history from the beginning of time He has kept and fulfilled His promises— and this one will be no different. You might say you can take it to the bank, and the bank of the Jordan may not be too far off in imagining.

But why is He not here? Why hasn't He yet come? Have we looked around at our world today? Wars upon wars and threats of wars. Moral depravity has taken over the minds not only of masses of people but in leadership as well. Who is seeking the Lord in guidance? Who is consulting with the Author and Creator of everything and His intentions of world order? We even see fragments of the church conforming to the misguided ways of the world. Personal and community relationships are broken. Some would even say it is scary times we live in, with the chaos that finds its way even into our homes. There is a sickness in our land that I believe is pervasive. But there is a remedy and a prescription prescribed by the Doctor who brought us into this world. It involves discipline on our part to take the medicine as prescribed and regularly administer the dosage to be made well. It involves a heart of humility in prayer, seeking the Doctor and His wisdom to heal, that a change would be evident in life itself. And we cry out, *Where is He? Why hasn't He come? "Come Lord Jesus," should we not pray?*

What is interesting is that there have been some, if not many who have proposed and predicted the actual time that our Lord will return and have proven that it was of their own mind and not that of the Lord. Our Lord Jesus says even the Son does not know the time and that it will be like a thief in the night, which encourages the faithful to continuously be prepared as if tonight was the night of reference:

"But concerning that day and hour no one knows, not even the angels of heaven, nor the Son, but the Father only. For as were the days of Noah, so will be the coming of the Son of Man." (Matt. 24:36-37)

Now concerning the times and the seasons, brothers, you have no need to have anything written to you. For you yourselves are fully aware that the day of the Lord will come like a thief in the night. While people are saying, "There is peace and security," then sudden destruction will come upon them as labor pains come upon a pregnant woman, and they will not escape. But you are not in darkness, brothers, for that day to surprise you like a thief. For you are all children of light, children of the day. We are not of the night or of the darkness. So then let us not sleep, as others do, but let us keep awake and be sober. (1 Thess. 5:1-6)

There will be one unassailable difference in that when our Lord came the first time, He came as a Lamb, a babe born in a manager virtually unnoticed by the world. A humble beginning to His earthly life, where little is known except for His mission commissioned by the Father with a mission of salvation for all who would believe in and of Him. When He returns, it will not be as a babe, for a babe is not born twice as some religions would postulate. Our faith, based on His sincerely spoken word when He repeats, "Truly, truly" for emphasis to listen, is secure in knowing that one must be born again, proving the transformation in belief. But this *born again* is not of the flesh but of the Spirit.

Jesus answered him, "Truly, truly, I say to you, unless one is born again he cannot see the kingdom of God." (John 3:3)

The difference in our Lord's next appearance will be noticed by the entire world, and it will be in the same way as He was watched going into heaven (Acts 1:11). The return will be beyond spectacular, as He will be accompanied with power and great glory as a Lion, unlike the Lamb of His first coming, and His mission will be judgment and a gathering of His children.

"Immediately after the tribulation of those days the sun will be darkened, and the moon will not give its light, and the stars will fall from heaven, and the powers of the heavens will be shaken. Then will appear in heaven the sign of the Son of Man, and then all the tribes of the earth will mourn, and they will see the Son of Man coming on the clouds of heaven with power and great glory. And he will send out his angels with a loud trumpet call, and

> *they will gather his elect from the four winds, from one end of heaven to the other." (Matt. 24:29-31)*

This is now the second letter that I am writing to you, beloved. In both of them I am stirring up your sincere mind by way of reminder, that you should remember the predictions of the holy prophets and the commandment of the Lord and Savior through your apostles, knowing this first of all, that scoffers will come in the last days with scoffing, following their own sinful desires. They will say, "Where is the promise of his coming? For ever since the fathers fell asleep, all things are continuing as they were from the beginning of creation." For they deliberately overlook this fact, that the heavens existed long ago, and the earth was formed out of water and through water by the word of God, and that by means of these the world that then existed was deluged with water and perished. But by the same word the heavens and earth that now exist are stored up for fire, being kept until the day of judgment and destruction of the ungodly. But do not overlook this one fact, beloved, that with the Lord one day is as a thousand years, and a thousand years as one day. The Lord is not slow to fulfill his promise as some count slowness, but is patient toward you, not wishing that any should perish, but that all should reach repentance. But the day of the Lord will come like a thief, and then the heavens will pass away with a roar, and the heavenly bodies will be burned up and dissolved, and the earth and the works that are done on it will be exposed. Since all these things are thus to be dissolved, what sort of people ought you to be in lives of holiness and godliness, waiting for and hastening the coming of the day of God, because

> *of which the heavens will be set on fire and dissolved, and the heavenly bodies will melt as they burn! But according to his promise we are waiting for new heavens and a new earth in which righteousness dwells. (2 Pet. 3:1-13)*

But the questions remain: Where is He, and why hasn't He yet come? Is it because of His love for everyone He has created, that none should perish into the abyss? Is He patient with us, proving an awaiting grace for us who linger in our own ways, waiting for that time when we awaken to the realization that we are on the wrong road? We know, or should know, that our Lord's plan and timing is perfect, and we can know that tomorrow, if it comes, we will be one day closer to when He comes than we are today. But to answer, *Where is He,* we can know that He is not far, He is not distant, and He is intimately closer to His creation than we could ever know. We can be secure in His promised presence and not grieve, for the joy of the Lord is our strength. And to answer, *Why hasn't He yet come,* we only need to heed to His own words:

> *But by His word the present heavens and earth are being reserved for fire, kept for the day of judgment and destruction of ungodly people. But do not let this one fact escape your notice, beloved, that with the Lord one day is like a thousand years, and a thousand years like one day. The Lord is not slow about His promise, as some count slowness, but is patient toward you, not willing for any to perish, but for all to come to repentance. (2 Pet. 3:7-9)*

Tomorrow for the Lord would be like a thousand years for us; so much for our understanding of time in the full wisdom of God. Incomprehensible? Yes, and so our best response is to enjoy Him through our days, knowing what He has told us: He loves us, and our good is His top priority. Sounds selfish, but that is because we lack the full wisdom of God and must rely on and trust in His word and His promises, and we can persevere for a short time, and then we will be with Him in what He has said is paradise. Keeping our eyes on things that are above and not on things on earth will give us the right perspective, the strength in knowing Him. He is our strength and our shield and has been for all who have heard His call from the beginning of time.

Is He coming? Yes! Is He here? Yes! And He has said blessed are we.

> *Blessed be the God and Father of our Lord Jesus Christ, who according to His great mercy has caused us to be born again to a living hope through the resurrection of Jesus Christ from the dead, to obtain an inheritance which is imperishable, undefiled, and will not fade away, reserved in heaven for you, who are protected by the power of God through faith for a salvation ready to be revealed in the last time. In this you greatly rejoice, even though now for a little while, if necessary, you have been distressed*

> *by various trials, so that the proof of your faith, being more precious than gold which perishes though tested by fire, may be found to result in praise, glory, and honor at the revelation of Jesus Christ; and though you have not seen Him, you love Him, and though you do not see Him now, but believe in Him, you greatly rejoice with joy inexpressible and full of glory, obtaining as the outcome of your faith, the salvation of your souls.*
> *(1 Pet. 1:3-9)*

Though the whole world denies Him, we remain steadfast and faithful, keeping His spoken and written Word in the greatest of love until the day when our faith becomes sight and our thanksgiving will be face to face.

> *For now we see in a mirror dimly, but then face to face; now I know in part, but then I will know fully, just as I also have been fully known. But now faith, hope, and love remain, these*

> *three; but the greatest of these is love.*
> *(1 Cor. 13:12-13)*

His promise remains and will be fulfilled; He is coming.

> *"And behold, I am coming quickly. Blessed is the one who keeps the words of the prophecy of this book." (Rev. 22:7)*

He has promised!

37

THE NEW OF THE NEW

What's *new?* is the question. Seems like nothing is new, and days grow in likeness and repeated are the things of yesterday. Even Solomon, the wisest man to walk this earth apart from Jesus our Lord, said, "There is what has been will be again, what has been done will be done again; there is nothing new under the sun."[107] So what is new? Well, there are some things that are, and we can start with God's faithful promise. His mercies are new every morning!

> *Because of the Lord's faithful love we do not perish, for His mercies never end. They are new every morning; great is Your faithfulness! (Lam. 3:22-23)*

Nothing new about His faithfulness, but we do find a need for mercy every day, even on the days we don't realize it. Do you find it interesting that everything finds the common denominator of everything about our Lord? An indiscriminate four-letter word: *Love.* His love for us.

Though everything may seem to remain the same and repeat itself in time, we can find the newness each day brings. It is a searching attitude, an attitude of gratitude, looking for the hidden and unhidden blessings. Looking for the good instead of the bad. We are bombarded with the negative, and eventually, for some, we fool ourselves into believing, finding the bad makes us feel good. We find that is a lie when we begin to peel back the layers of fraud that bundle the deception. It takes an intentional heart to battle against the schemes of the devil. Yes, I believe that the evil one is behind every deception and would have us join the ranks of bad company to console us into the corruptive mind to pridefully look for the argument, to look for others' faults, to build ourselves up on the misfortunes of others. The temptations are great, and we know who the master tempter is. We intentionally have to guard against the evil that would draw us into much company. Paul wrote in his first letter to the church in Corinth, "Be not deceived: 'Bad company corrupts good morals.'"[108]

Being aware of our fleshly weakness is a good start for a heart that yearns to obey. Our Lord recognizes this weakness and warns us against the temptations of the devil and gives us the protective strategy and godly tactic that He knows works: "Keep watching and praying that you may not fall into temptation; the spirit is willing, but the flesh is weak."[109]

Our Lord Jesus speaks from experience. He is not hypothesizing about what may or may not be appropriate in defense in such circumstances. He was tempted in every way. You can say the devil threw the book at Him. But Jesus threw the Book (He wrote) right back at Him. It is not wise to challenge an Author on a book He wrote. Though we are challenged seemingly every day in this same way, knowing the Author and the Book He wrote is wisdom He gives us changes the calculated odds against us to His favor.

Jesus was at His weakest physically but not mentally. He had fasted forty days and forty nights, which would leave the body yearning for sustenance; He would want to eat. The devil is pretty crafty, so the first thing he throws at Jesus in temptation is food. But the Lord isn't biting (ha!), and the prevailing word of the Lord leaves the devil searching for another channel of deceit because the validity of the first has been shattered into the abyss. We need to know that the devil is persistent when it comes to getting his way, and we need a formidable protector that is greater in us than he that is in the world.[110]

All this to keep on the bright side of things, looking for the good to enjoy the day, knowing we have a great God working for our good. So how do we intentionally look for the good? Let me use the body as an example—the body of a woman, because I am a man. Makes no difference, though; choose as you like.

Now this woman may be having a bad day, and by some circumstance you are brought into her presence. Her hair is really messed up, and she is not unlike most other women; hair is a big deal. Her clothes are tattered and torn, and it has been a while since she has been able to bathe. She is not in a good mood, and your initial instinct is to run and survive what may be a colossal defeat in agony. But you stay and are intentional about finding the good, and you look into her eyes, and they are beautiful. One cannot hide the gift of the eyes. When was the last time we looked into the eyes of someone we were talking to? I mean really looked into their eyes and gazed at them. If we have, we know that we got their attention, maybe questioning what we are doing or looking at. Well, we can tell them and exclaim what beautiful eyes they have, and suddenly, there is a change. I don't know what it is or how it is, but there is a change that is encouraging to move from negative thoughts to a brighter side that leads to the good.

I truly believe that we can always find the good if we want to. The temptation is to find the bad and dwell on it, and that is the evil one at our doorstep trying to pry open the door to let himself in. Let the word of the Lord keep that door locked, and every combination the devil tries will be the wrong sequence of numbers or keys.

What is the *new of the new* when everything seems the same? It is *us*. We are renewed in Spirit, purifying our hearts. What is the new of the new when nothing seems changed? It is Jesus, ready and willing to give us whatever is needed in life and godliness, supplying all our needs according to His glorious riches.[111] And He does not stop there, for coming is the *new of the new!* A promised new heaven and new earth.

"Then I saw a new heaven and a new earth; for the first heaven and the first earth passed away, and there is no longer any sea. And I saw the holy city, new Jerusalem, coming down out of heaven from God, prepared as a bride adorned for her husband. And I heard a loud voice from the throne, saying, 'Behold, the tabernacle of God is among the people, and He will dwell among them, and they shall be His people, and God Himself will be among them, and He will wipe away every tear from their eyes; and there will no longer be any death; there will no longer be any mourning, or crying, or pain; the first things have passed away.' And He who sits on the throne said, 'Behold, I am making all things new.' And He said, 'Write, for these words are faithful and true.'" (Rev. 21:1-5)

That is to come and is promised: all things will be made new. Though we wait, it is our hope and our faith that we can live right now in the new, knowing what is to come. So look into the eyes of Jesus, the beautiful eyes of Jesus, in everything, and you will notice a difference in everything and find the good that is always there.

ENDNOTES

PART 1

1 Rom. 12:1

2 Jer. 21:9

3 John 8:12

4 John 3:5

5 2 Pet. 3:4

6 2 Pet. 3:5

7 John 7:38

8 Matt. 19:21

9 John 14:1, 6

10 Matt. 16:24-26

11 1 Pet. 1:8

12 Matt. 6:33

13 Ps. 119:18

14 Rom. 8:14

15 Eph. 1:3

16 Eph. 1:13-14

17 John 10:27

18 Luke 3:2, 4

19 Dan. 4:31

20 Jer. 6:16

21 John 5:25

22   1 Kings 4:34

23   1 Pet. 1:13

24   Prov 1:33

25   Col. 3:2-4

26   Col. 2:8

27   2 Pet. 1:5

28   Eph. 5:1, 2

29   Rom. 12:1

30   2 Pet. 1:3

31   Henry Blackaby, *Experiencing God* (Brentwood, TN: B&H Books, September 1, 2008).

32   *The Complete Works of Oswald Chambers* © 2000 by Oswald Chambers Publications Association Limited. Used by permission of Our Daily Bread Publishing, P.O. Box 3566, Grand Rapids, MI 49501. Used with permission.

33   Oswald Chambers, *The Complete Works*.

34   John 8:32

35   John 15:5

36   John 21:19

37   John 21:21

38   John 21:22

39   *Complete Works*, p. 1,312.

40   Matt. 5:16

41   Zech. 4:6

42   1 Pet. 1:15-16

43   John 15:8

44   Exod. 3:4

45   Josh. 5:15

46   Josh. 5:14

47   From "The Importance of Holiness" course description, a Ligonier Ministries teaching series featuring R. C. Sproul.

48   Isa. 45:6

49   Luke 22:67-70

50   Matt. 15:16

51   John 4:25-26

52   Matt. 16:15-16

53   Listen to "His Name is Wonderful" by Audrey Mieir, © 1959, renewed 1987 by Manna Music, Inc.

54   Acts 2:38

55   Acts 3:16

56   Phil. 4:3

57   Rev. 13:8

PART 2

58   2 Pet. 1:3

59   Ps. 51:17

60   Matt. 6:6

61   Rom. 12:2

62   John 17:22-23

63   1 John 4:4 (note: this is not a direct quote, only a reference)

64   Phil. 2:3

65   Col. 1:22

66   Matt. 10:22-23

67   Matt. 10:24

68   Mark 12:31

69   Gal. 5:15

70   John 15:15

71   Luke 22:70

72   John 21:12

73   John 21:17

74   2 Chron. 7:14

75   Matt. 5:3, 5

76   Luke 18:7

77   1 Sam. 9:16

78   Ps. 18:2

79   2 Thess. 3:16

80   Ps. 46:7

81   Deut. 31:6

82   Isa. 35:3

83   Rom. 8:31

84   Phil. 4:13

85   Rom. 8:16-18

86   Acts 9:15-16

87   Heb. 11:1

88   1 Cor. 10:15-17

89   Isaac Watts, "Alas and Did My Savior Bleed," originally written in 1707. Public domain.

90   Concept from John B. Foley, S.J., "One Bread One Body," © 1978, John B. Foley, S.J., and OCP. All rights reserved.

PART 3

91   Gen. 1:27

92   Jer. 29:11

93   Col. 3:23

94   Isa. 48:9-11

95   2 Pet. 1:3

96   Listen to "I Will Call Upon the Lord" by Michael O'Shields, copyright Universal Music Corp. o/b/o Sound III, Inc. and Universal Music Corp.

97   Definition of *instrument* taken from Oxford Languages, https://search.yahoo.com/search?p=instrument&fr=yfp-t&fr2=p%3Afp%2Cm%3Asb&ei=UTF-8&fp=1

98   Exod. 3:5

99   Exod. 3:6

100 Matt. 10:27

101 Jer. 42:6

102 Luke 22:70

103 John 21:1-19

104 John 14:6

105 Ps. 51:17

106 Paraphrase of "There Shall Be Showers of Blessing,"
Daniel Webster, pseudonym Daniel W. Whittle, 1883.

107 Eccles. 1:9

108 1 Cor. 15:33

109 Matt. 26:41

110 1 John 4:4

111 2 Pet. 1:3; Phil. 4:19